By Larry McMurtry

By Larry McMurtry and Diana Ossana

In a
Narrow
Grave

ESSAYS ON TEXAS

Larry McMurtry

A TOUCHSTONE BOOK
Published by Simon & Schuster
New York • London • Toronto • Sydney • Singapore

 Rockefeller Center
1230 Avenue of the Americas
New York, NY 10020

Second Touchstone Edition 2001

Designed by Elina D. Nudelman

Manufactured in the United States of America

10   9   8   7   6   5   4   3   2   1

Library of Congress Cataloging-in-Publication Data

McMurtry, Larry.

In a narrow grave : essays on Texas / Larry McMurtry—2nd
Touchstone ed.

p. cm.

Originally published: Austin : Encino Press, 1968.

"A Touchstone book"

Includes bibliographical references (p.).

1. Texas—Civilization—20th century. 2. Texas—Social life and
customs—20th century. I. Title.

F391.2 M25 2001   2001020664
976.4'06—dc21
ISBN 0-684-86869-5

For information regarding special discounts for bulk purchases,
please contact Simon & Schuster Special Sales at 1-800-456-6798
or business@simonandschuster.com

For James;
& to the memory of Uncle Jeff & Uncle Johnny;
& for Ken Kesey, the last wagon master.

"By my father's grave there let mine be,
And bury me not on the lone prairie."

"Oh, bury me not—" And his voice failed there.
But we took no heed of his dying prayer;
In a narrow grave just six by three
We buried him there on the lone prairie . . .
                              —"The Dying Cowboy"

We beat the drum slowly
And shook the spurs lowly,
And bitterly wept
As we bore him along;
For we all loved our comrade,
So brave, young, and handsome,
We all loved the cowboy
Although he'd done wrong . . .
                              —"The Cowboy's Lament"

"I first took to drinking and then to card-playing"—
and they'd all be drunk when they was singing it,
most likely. Cowboys loved to sing about people
dying; I don't know why. I guess it was because
they was so full of life themselves . . .
   —Teddy Blue, We Pointed Them North

CONTENTS

A Preface

THIS FIRST COLLECTION of essays represented, for me, something in the nature of a pregnant pause. I had written, more or less in one motion, three short elegiac novels (*Horseman, Pass By; Leaving Cheyenne; The Last Picture Show*), all of which dealt in a small way with a large theme: the move from the land to the cities (or the small town to the suburbs), which occurred in so much of America shortly after World War II.

Before I was out of high school I realized I was witnessing the dying of a way of life—the rural, pastoral way of life. In the Southwest the best energies were no longer to be found in the homeplace, or in the small towns; the cities required these energies and the cities bought them. The kids who stayed in the country tended to be dull, lazy, cautious, or all three; those with brains, zip, and daring were soon off to Dallas or Houston.

I recognized, too, that the no longer open but still spacious range on which my ranching family had made its livelihood for two generations would not produce a livelihood for me or for my siblings and their kind. The cattle range had become the oil patch; the dozer cap replaced the Stetson almost overnight. The myth of the cowboy grew purer every year because there were so few actual cowboys left to contradict it.

The oil patch, curiously, has as yet produced no myth; the gaudy figure of the wildcatter goes only about as far as James Dean took it in *Giant*.

In the Foreword and Introduction which follow, written in 1968, when *In a Narrow Grave* was published, I say in essence what I've said above, and say it perhaps with a bit more poetry. In those days I had yet to grow weary of my own prose; I might live with a sentence through five or six drafts, whereas nowadays two are usually all I can stomach.

What I didn't know then was that I was about to leave not merely the land itself but also the rural point of view and, in a sense, the myth. As soon as the essays were published I set about writing a counterbalancing trio of novels (*Moving On*; *All My Friends Are Going to Be Strangers*; *Terms of Endearment*), which dramatized the same or similar experience from the urban point of view.

Excepting the Foreword and Introduction, only three of the essays were written specifically for the book: the ones on sex in Archer County, on Southwestern literature, and on my family. Looking through the volume now, I think that the essay I remain proudest of is the one on Southwestern literature. As a critical essay it is straightforward, if not pedestrian, but it does take the first hard look at those iconic figures Dobie, Webb, Bedichek. This was not merely useful, it was a necessary thing to do; the somewhat too earnest but reasonably energetic school of criticism which exists in Texas now owes something to that essay, although most of the critics themselves disagree with it.

I had actually been living in cities for fourteen years when I pulled together these essays; intellectually I had long been a city boy, but imaginatively I was still trudging up the dusty path that led out of the country. The essays were a sort of bridge: behind me lay the mystic plain, ahead the metropolis of the muses. I wanted to cross; I hope I have.

—*Larry McMurtry*
1989

A Foreword

IN HIS INTRODUCTION to *Cannibals and Christians*, Mr. Norman Mailer draws a succinct and provocative distinction between two sorts of writers who publish essay collections:

> The first kind writes sufficiently well to induce his publishers to put together his very separate pieces, and they are printed as a convenience to his readers. In such collections there is a tendency for the attitude to belong to the subject more than to the author—professional football is seen as professional football and ladies' fashion as ladies' fashion. The other kind of writer may be better or worse, but the writings always have a touch of the grandiose, even the megalomaniacal: the reason may be that the writings are parts of a continuing and more or less comprehensive vision of existence into which everything must fit. Of course, if the vision is interesting, the fit can be startling, dramatic, illuminating . . . but good or poor, the unspoken urge is to find secret relations between professional football and ladies' fashion and bring them in alive as partners to the vision . . .

Mr. Mailer, brilliant and durable *provocateur* that he is, naturally wants his own collections in the second category, and he devised, as long ago as 1959, a method of commentary—partly autobiographical, partly metaphoric—which functions as a sort of highly tensile intellectual baling wire, very useful to him when he wants to bring a cutting of essays out of the field and put them, as it were, in the literary barn. His method is well worth pondering, particularly if one is, as I am, a young writer about to publish a book of essays, all of which deal with a subject of less interest to literate Americans than either professional football *or* ladies' fashion: to wit, Texas.

Unfortunately, the essays I have published are so few and so local that no amount of commentary could bind them into an interesting bale. I should perhaps have left them to rot in the fields, but instead I have chosen to subsume them into a longer and (I hope) a larger work. For a time I thought it might be possible to stitch the individual pieces into a single lengthy essay, a seamless, well-cut aesthetic garment. Indeed, it might have been possible, but if so, I was not a good enough tailor. The garment that resulted is ragged and anything but seamless, and in a number of places the skin of my original subject has been left quite bare.

Nevertheless, though what follows is not a single essay, it is, I believe, continuous. My vision of existence is based almost entirely upon a prolonged scrutiny of West Texas and is probably too dry and flat; and I have no wish to be either grandiose or megalomaniacal. What I do claim is that the attitude in the following pages belongs to me, not to my subject. An interviewer once asked Mr. John Barth if it were true that there came a time in the creation of a novel when the characters suddenly rose up and took command of a narrative. Mr. Barth said no, but it was clear that the mere prospect of such a literary mutiny left him somewhat shaken. "Those rascals aren't going to get control if I can help it," he added staunchly. I feel much the same way about my subject here. I haven't spent thirty years in Texas just to be able to be objective about the place.

In the same interview Mr. Barth goes on to speculate that perhaps the novelist's basic motive is a desire to reinvent the world. A noble motive, surely, and never more so than now. Perhaps such a motive is no less noble when applied to smaller geographical units. If someone in the twenties had had a competent go at reinventing Texas, what might we be today?

In any case, I agree with Mr. Barth that the novel is a superb medium for such a reinvention—very probably the best medium that we have. For myself, the novel is a habitation; the essay is neither so familiar nor so constant. The essay is a place one visits occasionally, when one is tired of home. It offers the comforts of a fine hotel: one can stroll about in one's best clothes and ruminate upon all those things one never has time to ruminate upon at home. And what I generally find I am ruminating upon in the essay is home itself, the place where my characters live. I can never be quite sure whether home is a place or a form: the novel, or Texas. In daily life the two become crucially but vaguely related, and it is difficult to say with precision where place stops supporting fiction and fiction starts embodying place. One of the purposes of these essays is to investigate that relation, if only indirectly. I have a feeling I had better decide where I'm living before I do any more remodeling or reinventing.

IF I COULD SUMMON TWO writers from the Shades and set them the task of writing about this state, I think I would summon D. H. Lawrence and Machado de Assis. I would want Lawrence as he was in the early twenties, at about the time of *England, My England* or the *Studies in Classic American Literature*; Machado I would prefer in middle age, perhaps around 1880, when he was fed up with romantic convention and ready to write the *Epitaph of a Small Winner*. With Lawrence at his keenest and Machado at his driest and most deft, Texas would be had.

Of course if left around too long they both might end up

liking the place. Lawrence was susceptible to the primitive, Machado to the feudal; and a great many visiting sharp-shooters do end up liking Texas. One sees them here and there about the state, settled comfortably amid their chipped and shattered targets. At any rate, it is not always the aim one admires in Lawrence and Machado, it is the assurance with which they shoot. It is their authority, the clarity of their observations, and their quickness, here one paragraph, there the next. Such agility is enviable, and particularly so if one is setting out to write about Texas. Faced with such a task, one would like to be quick, clear, and agile; let a thought or a memory get a few yards head start and one might have to chase it halfway across the state. It is like roping in the brush country: if you don't catch the calf in the first clearing you may be in for a long and thorny pursuit.

In what follows I have been as succinct as possible, hoping to spare the reader thorns. At times I have been more than succinct—peremptory would be the accurate word. Much of the book is opinion, my opinion, and for the most part I have chosen simply to lay it out, garnished with a sliver of memory or the salt of metaphor. Pussyfooting is a vice I have been concerned to avoid.

It has come to my notice, however, that in these parts directness is frequently taken for malice. With that in mind, I might say at the outset that in criticizing Texas I have not been unaware that there are other states to which the same criticisms might apply. If so, that's dandy. I am sure there are potatoes in Nebraska, but Nebraska is not my rooting ground.

—*Larry McMurtry*
1968

An Introduction:
The God Abandons Texas

BEING A WRITER and a Texan is an amusing fate, one that gets funnier as one's sense of humor darkens. In times like these it verges on the macabre. Apparently there was a time in the forties and fifties when people sort of enjoyed reading about Texas, if the reading was light enough. The state was thought to be different—another country, almost. It had Nieman-Marcus and the Alamo and a lot of rather endearing millionaires. As late as 1961 Mr. John Bainbridge of *The New Yorker* was able to do well with a book called *The Super-Americans,* a collection of polite anecdotes about the millionaires. For Texas letters, the forties and fifties were the Golden Age; that is, J. Frank Dobie was still alive. To Texas readers he was a notch above Homer and a notch below Shakespeare, while the world outside reckoned him almost as good as Carl Sandburg. One moderately good writer was all that was expected of a place like Texas.

In those days, of course, Lyndon Johnson was still only half of Rayburn and Johnson. The nation's intellectuals lost no sleep over him, and *MacBird* was undreamt of.

Alas, all is changed. We aren't thought of as quaintly vulgar anymore. Some may find us *dangerously* vulgar, but the majority just find us boring. As a subject, Texas has become frankly stultifying: if it's another country, it's a country literate America hopes to hear no more about. That magisterial stream, the "Pedernales," is frequently pissed in now by intellectuals who appear to hope that the products of their literary bladders will somehow eat holes in the Presidential motorboat. Having yielded Mr. Johnson, it is hardly to be expected that the state will yield anything funny in the next few years, much less anything aesthetically interesting.

❦

THUS THE WRITER LIKE MYSELF, whose characters live in Texas, may find himself writing into a rather stiff wind. If he is ambivalent about the state as a place, the stiffness of the wind may cause him to become discouraged about it as a subject. This is particularly apt to happen if he attempts to write *from* Texas, as well as about it. Many Texas writers migrate, of course, and make their way to the literary capitals; there they often find their frontier manners and their experience in the boondocks so marketable socially that they have little time for reflection, and, indeed, little desire to reflect upon the place they have left. What most of them find the time for is nostalgia, a somewhat different thing.

It would be a pity if the chill literary winds discourage too many people about Texas as a subject, for present-day Texas is a very rich subject, particularly for the novelist. Present-day California might be even richer, but California, whether as a subject or a place to live, is almost too taxing. There the confusion is greater, the rivalries of manners more intense: the question is whether anyone can live in California and comprehend it clearly now. Nathanael West would have a harder time with the state today than he had in 1939.

Texas is almost as intense, but much less dizzying. Society here is divided, but it is not yet fragmented to a degree that would raise difficulties for the novelist. The state is at that stage of metamorphosis when it is most fertile with conflict, when rural and soil traditions are competing most desperately with urban traditions—competing for the allegiance of the young. The city will win, of course, but its victory won't be cheap—the country traditions were very strong. As the cowboys gradually leave the range and learn to accommodate themselves to the suburbs, defeats that are tragic in quality must occur and may be recorded.

✂

I STARTED, INDEED, TO CALL this book *The Cowboy in the Suburb*, but chose the present title instead because I wanted a tone that was elegiac rather than sociological. Nonetheless, I think it is essentially that movement, from country to subdivision, homeplace to metropolis, that gives life in present-day Texas its passion. Or if not its passion, its strong, peculiar mixture of passions, part spurious and part genuine, part ridiculous and part tragic.

However boring Texas might be to move to, it is not a boring place to be rooted. The transition that is taking place is very difficult, and the situations it creates are very intense. Living here consciously uses a great deal of one's blood; it involves one at once in a birth, a death, and a bitter love affair.

From the birth I expect very little: the new Texas is probably going to be a sort of kid brother to California, with a kid brother's tendency to imitation.

The death, however, moves me—the way of life that is dying had its value. Its appeal was simple, but genuine, and it called to it and is taking with it people whom one could not but love.

The last, the affair of the heart and blood, is really more physical than would have seemed possible, with a land so unadorned; but the quality of one's intimacy with a place seems to depend as little on adornment as the quality of one's intimacy with a woman. One should not, perhaps, call it a *bitter* love affair—merely one that has become a little too raw, too real, too stripped of fantasy. The time may have come to part or marry, but, for myself, I put no trust in either alternative. Parting would not leave me free, nor marriage make me happy.

There is a song Texas kids still sing, a song about the passing of the cowboy:

> *I'm going to leave*
> *Old Texas now,*
> *They've got no use*
> *For the longhorn cow.*
>
> *They've plowed and fenced*
> *My cattle range*
> *And the people there*
> *Are all so strange . . .*

It is a slight song, but, for the Texas writer, an inescapable subject. When I think about the passing of the cowboy, my mind inappropriately hangs on the poem of Cavafy's, from the scene in Shakespeare, from the sentence of Plutarch's: the poem in which the god abandons Antony. I like Cavafy's treatment best, with Antony at his window at night in Alexandria, bidden to drink past all deceiving while the god and his retinue file away. In Shakespeare only the guards hear the strange music that marks the god's departure, but it is still a telling moment—indeed, a telling fancy.

I can believe I have heard such music myself, in Fort Worth, Houston, Dallas; by the Rio Grande and the Brazos; in the brush country and on the Staked Plains. The music of departure is now rather faint, the god almost out of hearing. The god who abandoned Antony was Hercules—what is the name of the god who now abandons Texas? Sometimes I see him as Old Man Goodnight, or as Teddy Blue, or as my Uncle Johnny—all people the reader will meet if the reader reads on—but the one thing that is sure is that he was a horseman, and a god of the country. His home was the frontier, and his mythos celebrates those masculine ideals appropriate to a frontier.

Myself, I dislike frontiers, and yet the sense that my own has vanished produces in me the strongest emotion I have felt in connection with Texas, or with any place. It has embedded itself in the titles of each of my books, and just as I think I have worn the emotion out it seizes me again, usually at some unlikely moment. I see my son, age five, riding a mechanical horse in front of the laundromat on Sunday morning, and the sight calls up my Uncle Johnny, when *he* was age five, sitting on top of the McMurtry barn watching the last trail herd go by. It is indeed a complex distance from those traildrivers who made my father and my uncles determined to be cowboys to the mechanical horse that helps convince my son that he is a cowboy, as he takes a vertical ride in front of a laundromat.

That is the distance I hope to cover in this book. It may, like my other books, be a form of parting, a wave of the hand at Old Man Goodnight, Teddy Blue, Uncle Johnny and all they stood for.

❧

IT IS ALSO, ON A baser level, a literary gambit. It has clearly become necessary to write discursively of Texas if one is to be heard at all beyond one's city limits. The South, fortunately for its writers, has always been dark and bloody ground, but Texas is only scenery, and poor scenery at that. Even so, Mr. Faulkner had to write about a girl being raped with a corncob before he gained more than a semblance of a readership, and most of that soon deserted him. Today the fields of fiction are littered with raped bodies—try the corncob route and readers will yawn in your face.

As a regionalist, and a regionalist from an unpopular region, I find the problem of how to get heard rather a fascinating one. I haven't found it especially depressing, but then I wouldn't have gone in for writing if I hadn't liked talking to myself. I quite recognize that there have always been literary capitals and literary provinces, and that those who choose for whatever reason to abide in the provinces need not expect a modish recognition. Recently, of course, the picture has become much brighter. The Texas writer who really wants to get famous has only to work up his autobiography in such a way that it will (1) explain the assassination and (2) make it possible for President Johnson to be impeached. If he can do that, his name is made. *The New York Review of Books* will beat a path to his door, particularly if his door happens to be somewhere in Manhattan. Should his door be in Anarene, Texas, they will probably rely on the mails, but in any event he can put obscurity behind him. If he ever gets to New York he may even meet Susan Sontag.

I don't understand the assassination and I doubt that I can do anything about the President. My chances of meeting Miss Sontag are accordingly pretty slim and I might as well forget about it and go on and write a book about the place where my characters live.

I have a feeling I had better do it now, before the emotion I feel at the thought of the god becomes only the memory of an emotion. That god is riding fast away, and will soon be out of sight and out of hearing.

In a
Narrow
Grave

I should like to start this book with Hud and end it with my family, the McMurtrys. That may entail a passage from the unreal to the real, or it may entail the reverse. We shall see.

Here's HUD in Your Eye

IN 1961 I published a first novel called *Horseman, Pass By*, a title I felt sure the world would remember. To my surprise, the world quietly overlooked it, and even the few staunch friends who read the book seemed to experience the gravest difficulties with the title. Some called it *Horseman, Goodbye*, others *Horseman, Ride By*, still others *Passing the Horseman*. One colleague took to calling it *So Long, Horseman*, but since he customarily speaks of my second book, *Leaving Cheyenne*, as *Leaving El Paso* I have decided that perhaps his memory is unusually whimsical. The nadir was reached one day when a kind but dotty old lady asked me if I was the man who wrote *The Four Horsemen of the Alamo*.

One evening several months after the novel was published I was sitting in Ft. Worth eating my Sunday supper when the phone rang and an excited Hollywood voice informed me that Paramount Studios was about to film my book. The title, of course, would have to be changed—it was much too poetic. Could I suggest an alternate?

Offhand, I couldn't, but I cheerfully agreed to try. I had

begun to feel that my devoted readership deserved something simpler in the way of titles. A few weeks later Mr.
Lloyd Anderson, the genial Paramount location manager,
came to Texas to look for a film site. One evening over dinner I asked him if they had decided what the picture would
be called.

"Well, not definitely," he said, poking his steak with sud-
den embarrassment. "They're thinking of calling it *Wild
Desire.*"

After a moment of silence we went gamely on with our
meal. "Write them if you've got any suggestions," Mr.
Anderson said. "Don't hesitate. They'd be glad to get your
ideas."

❦

I MULLED THE MATTER OVER FOR a few days and then sent
Paramount a list of about a dozen titles; the best, as I recall,
was *Coitus on Horseback,* a title I had long hoped to fit onto
something. In the rush of production that and the rest of my
suggestions somehow got brushed aside—the next report I
had, Paramount was going to call it *Hud Bannon Against the
World.* At that point I decided to give up on titles and con-
centrate my hopes on the location committee.

If they weren't going to call it *Coitus on Horseback* I hoped
they might at least find it possible to make the film in Archer
County, where I was raised. Archer County is not particularly
scenic, but I was all primed to observe the impact of
Hollywood on my hometown. Black humour was just being
invented and I could think of no easier way to get in on it. Mr.
Anderson obligingly took pictures of Archer County all one
northerly winter day, but all he got for his trouble was frozen
hands and shots of several thousand denuded and uncine-
matic mesquites. Archer County clearly would not do.

In late March, 1962, Mr. Anderson informed me that a

location had been chosen near the town of Claude, in the Texas Panhandle. Claude (population 895) lies thirty miles southeast of Amarillo, a city I have always regarded as Ultima Thule. Most of the filming was to be done around an old, abandoned ranch house a mile or so from Claude, but the pasture scenes would be filmed near the hamlet of Goodnight, in the rugged country bordering the Palo Duro Canyon.

When I saw the locations I had to admit that Archer County had been fairly defeated. In addition to the topographic advantages, there was a certain fitness in having a film which was in some sense about the end of ranching filmed so near the place where Old Man Goodnight had established the first Panhandle ranch. Goodnight drove the first herd into the Palo Duro in 1876 and built the great JA, the cattle ranch whose present headquarters are only a few miles from where *Hud* was filmed. No doubt the Old Man—as he is still called in that country—would have been disgusted by *Hud* if he could have seen it, but then if he were ranching today he would scarcely need go to the movies to find things to disgust him. Certainly he left the mark of his personality on the Panhandle as no other man ever has or likely ever will. The local cowboys who worked around the movie set knew a great deal more about Charles Goodnight than they knew about Paul Newman or any other movie star.

Often, during lulls in the filming, as I watched the white June thunderheads roll southward over the plains, I thought of the Old Man—a vigorous, irascible, lonely figure. In that country, looking at the weathered ranch buildings or out across the grassy, shadow-flecked plains, it was easier to believe in the ghost of Old Man Goodnight than in the costume-department darling in huaraches and yellow silk shirt who crossed and recrossed one's path.

BECAUSE OF TEACHING DUTIES IN Ft. Worth I missed the first month of filming. I made the drive to Amarillo one evening in early June, a cool, windy evening with distant lightning and the rumble of spring thunder on the plains. Just before midnight I passed through Claude—its streets deserted, its houses dark. I didn't even slow down, there was only a yellow blinker light where the highway cuts across the main street, but I noticed as I passed through that the name on the water-tower had been changed: it read THALIA, the name of the imaginary town in my novels. It was one of the finer moments I've had as an author.

The cast and production crew were staying at the huge Ramada Inn in Amarillo. It was midnight or after when I drove up, but a stream of traffic was circling the motel like Indians supposedly circled wagon trains. I broke through only with difficulty and checked in. Two policemen were standing by the swimming pool, morosely watching the traffic.

"If it was teenagers I could see it," one said. "But it ain't. It's grown women too, hopin' Paul Newman will come out and dive off this here divin' board. Somethin' like this comes to town you find out just how crazy the public is."

It appeared that the two officers were supposed to keep the town women from swarming over the motel and breaking into the actors' bedrooms, a task they found spiritually wearying.

"I'd rather be out chousin' Meskins," one officer said. "You can't stop all these women. Funny thing is, I grew up in this town and I don't remember there being so many women around. I wouldn't a thought there was this many women in the whole Panhandle."

The other officer seconded that. Only the week before, for all their vigilance, a bulky matron had managed to get through Newman's window in the early morning, and after that he and Brandon de Wilde had shifted rooms every two or three days, to confuse enemy intelligence, as it were.

"Never seen anythang like it," one officer said.

I hadn't either, so we all three stood at the edge of the pool and watched the circling ladies for a while. Diversion is not to be sneezed at, in Amarillo.

❦

PARAMOUNT HAD RENTED A SMALL flotilla of cars to transport the crew to and from the set, and the next morning one was made available to me. A publicity man offered to be my guide. When we started out he was very cheerful, but on the way the sky began to cloud over and the man's mood darkened accordingly. Rain meant lost time, and time was selling for thirty thousand dollars a day.

We turned off the highway just south of Goodnight and were immediately stopped by a man with a walkie-talkie. The road was in camera, and since they were shooting, we would have to wait. The wait lasted an hour. We listened hopefully to the hum of the walkie-talkie and watched the thickening grey clouds spume toward us out of the northwest. Just as I thought we were about to be allowed in, the guard hurried over and hastily motioned us off the road. The movie people were coming out. A huge truck with a camera boom on it came first, followed closely by about thirty cars in tight formation. The dust they raised on the dry road was sufficient to obscure whatever celebrities may have been inside.

We followed, and happily managed to park before the interceptors with the walkie-talkies got set up. As luck would have it we parked only a few yards from the car containing Paul Newman and Brandon de Wilde. They had just fin-

ished a round-up scene and were dressed like working cowboys: brown chaps, spurs, dusty boots, Levi jackets, and
well-broken-in straw hats.

Their dress was perfectly authentic, indistinguishable
from that of the dozen or so real cowboys who worked as
extras in the cattle scenes, but even so they didn't particularly look like cowboys. De Wilde looked like someone a millionaire oil man might invite to his ranch for a weekend. He
was enjoying the fantasy that he was a real cowboy, a man
of the soil, but he walked like a young executive, and
showed no hint of the characteristic slouch most cowboys
adopt when they are afoot. On a horse he was even worse,
as the film abundantly documents.

Newman came a great deal closer. He had picked up the
cowboy's habit of cocking one hip higher than the other
when he was standing still, and one could almost have taken
him for a young, aggressive rancher, someone just beginning to make his pile. One could have, perhaps, had it not
been for his eyes. His look was introspected and self-
occupied, though not egotistical; he simply looked more
curious about himself than most young ranchers look.

In the next hour I met a great many movie people, but
the only ones from that hour that I remember well were
Martin Ritt, the director, and Harriet and Irving Ravetch,
the screen-writers. I am not sure how I expected to be
greeted, but I was certainly ill-prepared for the barrage of
apologies I faced. For the first two hours no one did anything but apologize to me, presumably because they had
wrought changes in my book. I had quite expected the
changes and didn't care at all—by that time I didn't think
much of the novel anyway. I told them as much, but no one
seemed to believe me, and my mild assurances of good will
merely served to increase the general uneasiness at having
an author on the set. I think they would have welcomed

some display of temper. As it was, my quiet confusion was taken for Olympian disdain.

🦥

FORTUNATELY, LUNCH SOON CAME AND everyone loosened up a bit. The Ravetches and I made our way to the end of the chow line and were soon joined by Newman, who had a copy of a Durrenmatt play in his hand. Harriet Ravetch was attempting to protect herself from the wind and the abrasive dust with a formidable hat and a curtain of scarves; she succeeded rather well, but others were suffering considerably. Most of the crew had adopted the dress of the region; only the art director could have been considered satorially eccentric. He wore high-topped safari boots, heavy duck clothing, and an Australian bush hat.

Lunch was served each day by the late Walter Jetton of Ft. Worth, who was soon to become barbecuer to the President. Whatever one may think about Mr. Jetton's barbecue, his organization had to be admired: the 110-man crew plus guests were stuffed with professional dispatch. The fare was a sort of family-reunion special: pinto beans with chili pepper, potato salad, beef, chicken, ribs, ham, coleslaw, stewed apricots, cobbler, iced tea and coffee. Tables were ranged along the long porch of the old ranch house, and people ate there or on the ground. Those so fastidious as not to like Panhandle sand in their iced tea ate inside the house, which was completely bare except for a table piled with photographs.

I have no fondness for sand and chose to eat inside. There was no place to sit, so I stood up and idly looked through the stills as I ate. I noticed there seemed to be an awful lot of photographs of buzzards, and when I went outside to get some more beans I asked the Ravetches how the buzzard scene had turned out. I had merely thought to make conver-

header: Larry McMurtry

sation and was a little taken aback by the number of stricken looks that turned my way. "Oh, those fucking buzzards," someone said, in a tone that discouraged further discussion.

Later I managed to get a version of the buzzard story from some extras, who thought it hilarious. There was to be a scene in which a number of buzzards sit around waiting for the people to leave so they can consume a dead heifer. Newman roars up and in his wild way shoots one of the buzzards, whereupon the others fly away. The first difficulty turned out to be getting the buzzards. There are no professional buzzard-trappers in the Panhandle, and the few birds that showed up of their own accord were skittery and unphotogenic. It was necessary to arrange for someone in the vicinity of Laredo, roughly a thousand miles away, to round up a dozen buzzards and fly them by jet to Amarillo. The plan was to wire the buzzards to a dead tree until they had been photographed; then when Newman shot the gun they could be released electronically and photographed again as they soared into the blue Panhandle sky.

In outline it was a good plan, but it quite failed to take into account the mentality of buzzards. As soon as they were wired to the tree they all began to try and fly away. The wires prevented that, of course, but did not prevent them from falling off the limbs, where they dangled upside down, wings flapping, nether parts exposed. It is hard to imagine anything less likely to beguile a movie-going audience than a tree full of dangling buzzards. Everyone agreed it was unaesthetic. The buzzards were righted, but they tried again, and with each try their humiliation deepened. Finally they abandoned their efforts to fly away and resigned themselves to life on their tree. Their resignation was so complete that when the scene was readied and the time came for them to fly, they refused. They had had enough of ignominy; better to remain on the limb indefinitely. Buzzards are not without patience. Profanity, fire-crackers, and even a shotgun full of rock salt failed to move them. I'm told that, in desperation, a bird man was flown in from L.A. to teach the sulky bastards how to fly. The whole experience left everyone touchy. A day or so later, looking at the pictures again, I noticed a further provocative detail. The dead heifer that figured so prominently in the scene was quite clearly a steer. When I pointed this out to the still photographers they just shrugged. A steer was close enough; after all, they were both essentially cows. "In essence, it's a cow," one said moodily. No one wanted those buzzards back again.

❦

AS IT HAPPENED, I WAS not the only McMurtry connected with *Hud*. The cattle used in the film belonged to my cousin Alfred, whose ranch adjoined the land where the film was made. During the many lulls in shooting I visited with Alfred and his cowhands, hoping to find out how the cowboys reacted to the whole thing. It is not every day that cowboys get the chance to assist in creating an illusion about themselves.

When I first arrived, the cowhands were all looking forward to a scene in which Brandon de Wilde was to be kicked into a fence by a cow. De Wilde's stand-in was the one who would actually be kicked, a local boy whom all the cowboys knew. He was not exactly unpopular, but it was clear that the men thought stardom had gone to his head a bit—getting kicked through a fence ten or fifteen times would probably do him good.

On the whole, the cowhands derived a great deal of amusement from the film-making. They got on famously with the production crew, most of whom were as down-to-earth as they were. The hierarchy—stars, director, screen-writers—they regarded with tolerant incredulity. They clearly felt that what was going on was beyond the reach of ordinary human comprehension, and were consequently as diffident as they would have been with a company of Martians. "I'm just working from the shoulders down," one said, summing it up for them all.

On the third day of my visit a scene was prepared in which the cattle were put through the chutes and vaccinated. To hold them for inspection, the movie-makers were proposing to use a device called a dehorning gate—a heavy gate with a number of levers and bars which lock an animal's head firmly in place. A dehorning gate is painful enough for cattle, but it is far deadlier to the man who operates it, unless the man is an expert. He must catch the thrashing animal at just the right moment as it emerges from the chute; if his timing is off and the animal kicks just right the operator may catch one or both levers in the face. Even experienced gate men miss every now and then, and a broken jaw is one of the milder results. The movie-makers, unaware of this danger, were planning to have Paul Newman operate the levers himself. De Wilde could much more safely have been kicked through the fence a few times. The cowboys all knew this, but none of them made a move to mention it to the director. I mentioned it to him, and when I asked the cowboys why they hadn't, they just shrugged. Ritt was the *director*. For all they knew he *wanted* Newman to get hit in the jaw.

Like most visitors to a film-set, I soon discovered that my curiosity about filming was more limited than I would have supposed. It seemed a slow, repetitious, tedious business, no more so to me than to the people engaged in it. Except for Martin Ritt and James Wong Howe, almost everyone connected with the movie seemed bored. Half the crew was always inactive, and this half spent its time in one of the equipment sheds, gossiping, drinking coffee, gawking and being gawked at, and talking about sex. Ritt and Howe were the only two whose attention was fully and continuously engaged by the filming: the rest killed what time there was to kill as best they could. Newman did it most sensibly, by staying in his dressing room and reading. Others did it by titillating the crowd of local visitors. De Wilde practiced riding. Melvin Douglas reminisced about the stage.

The fellow who got the biggest kick out of dazzling the locals was a sort of Westian cowboy, a lineal descendant of Earl Schoop in *The Day of the Locust.* His mannerisms were updated and his idiom was closer to Stoney Burke than William S. Hart, but he was still very clearly a marginal man—a creature of the fringe. His nickname was S.C. (for Super Cock), and his stock-in-trade was sex. He talked, thought, knew nothing else. He had an official position, but I never saw him exercise it. Had it not been for his ability to keep the idle members of the crew amused, he would have been dead weight.

Whether his nickname flattered him I cannot attest, but I did observe that he had a way with women: he might not have been able to take them in, but he could certainly draw them out. Several times I saw him introduce himself to a group of farm women, none of whom had probably uttered ten words about sex in their entire lives. His candor seemed to hypnotize them; doubtless in their experience it was unprecedented. Within twenty minutes he would have them talking about their orgasms, those of them, at least, who had had any to talk about. Many were put on the defensive and found themselves attempting to defend their husband's performances, an awkward and unaccustomed task. Whatever the defense, S.C. always managed to be pleasantly derisive, pointing out to this or that little lady that she probably lacked a valid standard of comparison.

Later, in Hollywood, I saw S.C. lurking outside the studio in a four-year-old car, waiting to try his luck with the secretaries when they emerged at five o'clock. He looked much diminished. To the little ladies of Los Angeles he was just another cowboy shirt.

In Texas, as a general rule, money comes into the conversation much oftener than sex: on the movie set the reverse prevailed. Millions were being spent, but were seldom mentioned. Sex got mentioned constantly—the tedium of location work had to be relieved some way. At one point we were out on the plains shooting a scene with two longhorns when a heavy rain shower hit. Everyone piled into cars to wait for it to pass over, and I landed in a car with Martin Ritt and several of the actors. Someone mentioned a Richard Burton doll, the latest in Hollywood toys. You wound it up and it did incredible things to Elizabeth Taylor. This reminded someone of something that lady was rumoured to have done during the filming of *Giant,* which in turn reminded someone else of a disease Marlon Brando was rumoured to have caught in Tahiti, while doing *Mutiny on the Bounty.* Things went on in this vein for several minutes and I suddenly noticed that the back of the driver's neck had grown very red. I don't know what spades are called in California, but I have noted that the copulative act is usually called fucking, mixed company or no. We were mixed company, and the driver, a local man, was most probably a deacon in the Baptist church. None of the movie people even noticed that he had turned red.

On this particular day, Brandon de Wilde was feeling gloomy. It was clear that he was struggling hard to leave adolescence behind, but it wasn't always clear whether he was winning or losing. The most distasteful part of moviemaking, he complained, was that strange women kept trying to crawl in bed with him. He was an engaged man, and he had scruples. Some locations were worse than others: during the filming of *All Fall Down* his scruples had been overcome some eighteen times. A nightmare. A colleague unkindly pointed out that his scruples were of about the consistency of toilet paper, but I don't think de Wilde heard him. He was trying to decide whether to fly to El Paso that weekend, to test his scruples against the fleshpots of Juarez.

❦

I WAS ONLY AROUND THE set a few days, but that was quite long enough. The presence of the Californians set the life of the Panhandle in an odd perspective, one that I won't soon forget. I remember the stringy, hard-handed farm women giggling at S.C.'s indecencies; the solid, silent driver turning red; the wives and daughters of Amarillo, circling the Ramada Inn at night. In retrospect, the reactions seem perfectly predictable. The men of the area felt directly threatened: here was an energy and a masculinity that seemed stronger than their own. Women, on the other hand, felt expectant. Hollywood with all its money and its possibility was finally there. Anything might happen. Their leaden lives might be made golden, somehow.

When the movie was released, West Texas reacted ambivalently, but along much these same lines. It was said to be profane, and members of the hard-shell sects stayed away. A lady of my acquaintance offered to stay home and pray for her family while they went. Despite its taint, a great many people did go see it, and most of them came away enthusiastic. It was generally regarded as an accurate, even flattering picture of the area. The Panhandle preened itself for a time, and a baby or two was named Hud.

Any number of people assured me they knew someone just like Hud. *Their* Hud was a real hellion, they told me—if they were men their tone indicated that he was the sort of man they almost wished they had been: tough, capable, wild, undomesticated.

Invariably they would hasten to add that, so far as acting went, Melvyn Douglas took the cake. Hud might tempt them, but they knew well enough that old Homer was the sort of man their fathers had wanted them to be. Hud had made terms with the twentieth century, whereas Homer was unwaveringly faithful to the nineteenth, and in those parts the nineteenth century ideal has not yet lost its force. That Homer was a dreadfully sentimentalized version of the nineteenth century cattleman was apparently never noticed, except by Pauline Kael. Her excellent essay provides all that is needed in the way of criticism of *Hud*.*

If the men of the area wavered and were ultimately unable to identify either with Homer or with Hud, the women had no such problem. Most of them probably identified with the unseen woman whose bed Hud leaves when the movie opens. You don't find many Texas women willing to identify with a ranch cook, not even one that looks like Patricia Neal. Women seldom mentioned Miss Neal to me until after her illness, when tragedy had placed her clearly in a domestic context.

꿏

TO DATE I HAVE SEEN *Hud* six times, twice on my own and four times due to circumstances beyond my control. One showing was a bit unusual: it was to a college film group and the young projectionist had neglected to bring his cinemascope adjuster. Since the screen was only twelve feet wide the distortions that resulted were bizarre. The verticals were elongated, the horizontals squashed. Hud's Cadillac became

---

* *I Lost It at the Movies*, pp. 78–94.

a fat Volkswagen. The beautiful proportions were lost and one was left with nothing but the drama.

The sixth time around I decided I couldn't bear to watch it again, so I sat outside and listened. Again, I was left with the drama.

Those two showings did much to bring home to me what was excellent in the film and what was poor. The camera work of James Wong Howe was very fine, and the acting of Newman and Miss Neal equally so. The camera was completely faithful to the beauty and pitilessness of the Panhandle: it showed what is there, a land so powerful that it is all but impossible to live on it pleasantly. Newman and Miss Neal took advantage of their roles as brilliantly as the camera took advantage of the terrain; between them they saved what was otherwise a weak and badly shaped dramatic vehicle.

The first time I saw the film I thought the screenplay was superb. All I heard was the wit, and there is wit. By the third showing I had begun to wince, and by the sixth it seemed to me clear that the screen-writers had erred badly in following my novel too closely. *Horseman, Pass By* has its moments, but they do not keep it from being a slight, confused, and sentimental first novel. The screen-writers had the good sense to shift the focus from Lonnie to Hud, but otherwise they were content to follow the book, and as a result most of the confusion and all of the sentimentality were carried over. Touches which were overpoetic in the novel become merely awkward in the screenplay; occasionally a line of description from the book would be turned into a line of dialogue, but with no change in the adjectives, a practice hardly recommendable. Worst of all, they chose to stick with the novel's faulty structure, which meant that old Homer collapsed as pathetically and unconvincingly in the movie as he had in the book.

Still, I am grateful to the screen-writers for inadvertently pointing out to me where my story should have gone; and I am even more grateful to them for bringing home to me how careful one must be of the lyric impulse when writing about the Southwest. Prose, I believe, must accord with the land. The forests of East Texas reach to Yoknapatawpha— someone like William Humphrey can occasionally get away with the Faulknerian density. For the West, it doesn't work. A viny, tangled prose would never do for a place so open; a place, to use Ross Calvin's phrase, where the sky determines so much. A lyricism appropriate to the Southwest needs to be as clean as a bleached bone and as well-spaced as trees on the llano. The elements still dominate here, and a spare, elemental language, with now and then a touch of elegance, will suffice. We could probably use Mark Twain, but I doubt we're yet civilized enough to need a Henry James.

❦

SINCE THE MOVIE WAS RELEASED, I have not been through the town of Claude. I imagine they have put the correct name back on the water-tower, and now the name THALIA is on no water-tower anywhere. In June, though, the thunderheads will still roll south, across the JA and the Palo Duro; and in Claude and Clarendon, Muleshoe and Quitaque (Kitty-quay) the old-timers at their whittling still tell stories of the Old Man, Charles Goodnight. The stories slowly alter, become local myths. Some remember that the Indians called him Buenas Noches. They can tell the sad story of the last running, about the ragged band of Comanches who came all the way from their reservation in Oklahoma to Goodnight's ranch on the Quitaque, to beg a buffalo of him. At first he refused, but in time he relented and gave them a scrawny young bull, thinking they would drive it back to the reservation and eat it. Instead, whipping up their thin, miserable ponies, they ran it before him and killed it with lances and arrows, then sat looking at it for a time, remembering glories and centuries gone.

Such a story catches a whole people's loss, but only a few old men and a few writers tell it today,* and the old men, for that matter, usually tell it as a story about the craziness of Indians.

The Old Man has become a local god, his legends recounted in a few ranch houses, a few courthouses, and the domino parlors of a few West Texas towns. The old-timers and the cowboys know about him, but the youngsters of Texas don't; they know Hud, that keen, hard, attractive bastard who drives a Cadillac. Since the youngsters have never heard of the Old Man they don't know that Hud is his descendant, and the few who know both are so partisan to the Old Man that they would adamantly deny that the two are related. But related they are, though they knew different times, and put their powers to different uses.

๛

BEFORE I AM QUIT WITH Hud I want to make the lines of relation a bit clearer. I might add that I should be embarrassed to talk so much about one of my own characters, particularly a none-too-successful character from an early book, were it not that the Hud I am talking about is essentially the creation of the film. Insofar as he has an archetypal or mythological dimension, he is not my creation but relates to that myth of the Westerner which the movies themselves have helped create. The purpose of the section which follows is to relate that myth to the diverse rites from which it grew.

---

* See John Graves, *Goodbye to a River*, pp. 62–63.

Cowboys, Movies, Myths, & Cadillacs: An Excursus on Ritual Forms in the Western Movie

SINCE *HUD* WAS made I have often been asked if I think movies and television portray the American cowboy as he really is—or, to be more accurate, as he really was. The people who ask that question not only expect me to answer in the negative, but also obviously hope that I will then take Hollywood to task for its irresponsibility. To them, realism is something more than a method: it is a moral imperative. Similitude equals Truth equals Art. That is, of course, a very low-grade aesthetic, but it is one that crops up all too often. In this day and age everything is taken seriously, even the Western. People seem to want it to become a responsible genre.

I suppose I am as fond of responsible genres as the next man, but I am by no means sure I want the Western to become one. Until I read Robert Warshow's celebrated essay on the Westerner,* I had been quite content to think of the Western as simply a mode of entertainment, a mode

---

* *The Immediate Experience*, pp. 135–54.

in which the only "real" things were the horses and the land-scapes. I used Westerns as I might use the Maciste movies, as a means of disengaging myself from life for a couple of hours. I am seldom in the mood to look down my nose at a cheap, convenient escape, and even seldomer in the mood to wonder whether the escape is Art.

The kind of escapes one chooses are significant, no doubt, but our culture offers such a variety now that one's curiosity about them is apt to be blunted. Years ago, when I still lived on a ranch, I used to notice that there was a certain lack of similitude in Hollywood's treatment of cowboy life, but at that time I couldn't have cared less. The cowboys I knew couldn't have cared less, either. The only gaucherie I can remember them mentioning is what one might call the trotting-cattle syndrome, a very recurrent screen phenomenon. The moviegoer usually sees cattle being driven across the screen at a pace so rapid that even the wiriest Longhorn could not have sustained it the length of Hollywood Boulevard without collapsing. The trail herds of the seventies and eighties were grazed along at a sedate eight to ten miles a day—anything faster would have been economically disastrous.

❦

WARSHOW, OF COURSE, WAS RIGHT in pointing out that the working cowboy has never been very important in the Western movie. The Gunfighter has been the central figure, and cowboys and gunfighters were very different types, neither very good at the other's specialties. A Western may start out with a cowboy hero, but nine times out of ten the plot will require him to learn gunfighting, so that Right may prevail. Recently there have been signs that this is changing, especially on television. Domestic Westerns have become very popular (*Bonanza, The Big Valley,* even, I should say,

Gunsmoke), whereas the best of the gunfighter series—*Paladin*—is seen no more. (Neither, however, is *Rawhide*, the series which did the most with the working cowboy.)

Certainly, though, the effectiveness of the Western as a genre has never depended upon realism. The Winning of the West is a romantic subject—doing the cowboy realistically would have amounted to a sort of alchemical reverse English: it would have meant turning gold into lead. As a figure of high romance, the cowboy has remained compelling. He has outlasted the noble redman, Johnny Reb and Billy Yank, G.I. Joe, and any number of sports kings and entertainers. He successfully absorbed the figure of the pioneer, and with luck may even outlast acid-rock.

Still, the appeal can't last forever. The West definitely has been won, and the cowboy must someday fade. Indeed, a certain change has already taken place, and was taking place when Warshow wrote his essay (1954). If one can apply to the Western the terminology Northup Frye develops in his essay on fictional modes, we might say that in the fifties the Western began working its way down from the levels of myth and romance toward the ironic level which it has only recently reached. Westerns like *Shane, The Searchers,* and *Warlock* are in the high mimetic mode, with the hero still superior to other men and to his environment. In *The Gunfighter* this is not the case—we have moved to the low mimetic. *Welcome to Hard Times* is a recent example of the low mimetic Western; so, for that matter, is *Hud*, though it tends at several points toward the ironic. There are comparable developments in fiction: Thomas Berger's *Little Big Man* is a brilliant ironic performance. It's nearest cinematic equivalent is *Cat Ballou,* in which Lee Marvin won an Oscar for a role that parodies the Gunfighter.

No doubt high mimetic Westerns will continue to be made as long as John Wayne is acting—he wouldn't fit in any other mode—but in number they are declining, and the figure of the Westerner is gradually being challenged by more modern figures. At the moment, the Secret Agent seems to be dominant. In time, of course, we can expect to see the conquest of space (if we really conquer it) take over the place in the American mythos now held by the winning of the West, but that day has not yet come. If one agrees with Warshow (and I do) that one of the reasons the Western has maintained its hold on our imagination is because it offers an acceptable orientation to violence, then it is easy to see why the Secret Agent is so popular just now. An Urban Age demands an urban figure: the Secret Agent is an updated Gunfighter. James Bond has appropriated the skills of the Gunfighter and added urbanity and cosmopolitanism. Napoleon Solo and Matt Dillon both work for the betterment of civilization, but the Man from U. N. C. L. E. makes the Marshal seem as old-fashioned and domestic as Fibber McGee and Molly. In the former the violence, besides being aestheticized, has been brought into line with the times. If only there are some bad Indians out there in space, on a planet we need, then eventually the Spaceman's hour will come.

❧

The cowboy's golden age was the last third of the nineteenth century. In treating the golden age, Hollywood has been fairly effective, but what happened in the West after that age ended has so far barely been touched. The pictures which deal with it most directly are *Hud* and *Lonely Are the Brave.*

Hud, a twentieth century Westerner, is a gunfighter who lacks both guns and opponents. The land itself is the same—just as powerful and just as imprisoning—but the social context has changed so radically that Hud's impulse to violence is turned inward, on himself and his family. He is wild in a well-established tradition of Western wildness that involves drinking, fighting, fast and reckless riding and/or driving, and, of course, seducing. The tradition is not bogus. From the first the cowboy was distinguished for his daring and his cheerful indifference to middle-class values, and if present-day cowboys are more solidly middle-class than their ancestors were it is because their range is now gone and middle-classness is all but unavoidable. Cowboys know it, and comment on it in tones of regret. "I'm gettin' spoilt," they say ruefully, discussing some new softness their wives have got them to adopt. The tone is always joking, but it carries a sense of loss; how many years before they journey from their comfortable reservations in the suburb to beg of some old man a symbolic buffalo?

Hud, of course, is not simply a cowboy—if he were he could never afford the Cadillac. The Cadillac is his gun, in a sense, and it is a well-chosen symbol. One might note that the two best movies about the mid-twentieth century cowboy both end with the death of animals: the two Longhorns in *Hud* and the mare Whiskey in *Lonely Are the Brave*. Whiskey, most appropriately, is run over by a truck: it is trucks, not horses, that move cattle from Texas to Kansas these days.

The men of the West once related very strongly to animals; Roy Bedichek treats the subject beautifully in *Adventures With a Texas Naturalist*.* Now they are beginning to relate to machines. We see Hud on horseback only twice; we think of him in the Cadillac, a machine which has

---

* *Adventures With a Texas Naturalist*, p. 80–81.

a dual usefulness, just as the gunfighter's gun once had. It is both a symbol of status and a highly useful tool. But Hud is a rancher, not simply a cowboy. The cowboy could no more afford Hud's car than he could afford Hud's women, though the latter might vary considerably in expensiveness. Indeed, there has always been an element of asceticism in the cowboy's makeup: his binges seldom provide more than a night's relief from the hard, Spartan conditions of his life.

Along with the asceticism go pride, stoicism, directness, restlessness and independence, all characteristics which the cowboy expresses through his own astringent humour. This humour has seldom been touched, either in fiction or on the screen. Hud's wit was closer in idiom to the hard-boiled dick than to the cowboy, and in Westerns this is generally the case. The cowboy's temperament has not changed much since the nineteenth century; it is his world that has changed, and the change has been a steady shrinkage. There are no more trail herds, no more wide open cattle towns, no longer that vast stretch of unfenced land between Laredo and Calgary. If the modern cowboy is footloose, there is only the rodeo circuit, for most a very unsatisfactory life. Rodeo was given one excellent low mimetic treatment (*The Lusty Men*, 1952), but except for *Stoney Burke* and the rodeo sequence of *The Misfits* has hardly been touched since. The big western ranches are gradually breaking down into smaller and smaller ranches, and with the advent of pickups and horse trailers it is no longer necessary to spend weeks on the roundup. The effect of this has been to diminish the cowboy's isolation, his sense of himself as a man alone. From solitude and the clarity solitude sometimes brings he is being drawn toward the confusions of the urban or suburban neighborhood.

Also, unhappily, the cowboy's life is umbilically joined to a dying mother: the American range-cattle industry. I think again of Hud and Old Man Goodnight. If the Old Man were Hud's age today, what would he do? He might make a fortune, and he might achieve something great, but he wouldn't do either with cattle—not unless he chose to go to Australia or Brazil or the Argentine. If the Old Man were ranching now the frustration it would entail might cause him to waste his force in the same ways Hud wastes his. And Hud, given a frontier, might become a Charles Goodnight.

THE COWBOY'S GRADUAL METAMORPHOSIS INTO A suburban-ite is not without its element of paradox. The living conditions that make the wild, free cowboy such an attractive fantasy-figure to those already urbanized will eventually result in his being absorbed by his audience. In a sense this has already happened: nobody watches TV Westerns as avidly as cowboys. Even in his golden days the cowboy lived within the emotional limits of the Western movie and the hillbilly song. It was not pure frivolity that prompted me to appropriate Gilbert Murray's title for this chapter, but the belief that the central motifs of the Western movie relate to the simple pantheism of the cowboy, and the rituals of his life, in a way that makes the appropriation valid. Most central of all, I think, is the Ride, and the sacramental relationship of man and horse, matters which I will return to later.

For the moment, it is enough to observe that Hud is one of the many people whose capacities no longer fit their situations. He needs more room and less company, and is unlikely to get either. In West Texas a cow needs twenty or thirty acres of range to keep her nicely, and that's range at its best. Human generations will be needing those acres someday. The ranches will shrink to California size and the cattle will get raised in feedlots, thirty head to the acre, meals around the clock. The descendants of the trail-hands will be driving beer trucks in the suburbs of Ft. Worth, Dodge City, Cheyenne and a score of other cities whose names once held a different kind of promise.

※

THE COWBOY'S HUMOUR, FOR THOSE who have not been exposed to it, is a humour of aphorism, of ironic understatement. One should, then, be especially careful not to overstate his decline. The passing of the cowboy's day has produced personal tragedy, of course, but collectively his decline has been merely poignant. Compare it with that of the Indian, for example: almost any suburb looks good if the alternative to it is an Indian reservation. The cowboy has been diminished, but the Indian was destroyed. The great homeward march of the Northern Cheyenne in 1878 is a subject for a Sophocles, and was lucky to draw even a John Ford (*Cheyenne Autumn*). The cowboy's trouble will take a lighter handling, of the sort it is getting now. In time Hollywood will grow tired of parodying the Gunfighter and the ironic will yield to the mythic again; the Italian-made Clint Eastwood films (*A Fistful of Dollars* and sequels) mark, already, the reappearance of the archetype. Hud may leave the ranch forever and become an executive or an astronaut, but Gary Cooper will be back, perhaps as he was in *The Plainsman*—a figure of romance as remote and appealing as King Arthur.

※

FOR A MORE INSTRUCTIVE LOOK at the methods by which the myth of the Westerner is being made usable to the artist, one should have to turn from the film to literature. Filmmakers seldom own themselves; many might like to be serious but few are. Ultimately, the Western is *not* a responsible genre. Within the last twenty-five years the writers of the

West have done more with the mythic materials than film-makers have done, though unfortunately the work of most Western writers reaches only a limited audience and has only a limited impact. The film, if only because of its distribution and the power it achieves through pure repetition, continues to carry the myth to the mass audience.

An investigation of the recent literature of the West is beyond my competence, but I would like, before I quit the subject, to relieve myself of a few opinions about the literature of my own state.

Southwestern Literature?

TERRY SOUTHERN IS quite clearly the best writer ever to emerge from Alvarado, Texas, but is it possible that the Lone Star State inspired *Candy?* I fear not. Katherine Anne Porter was born in Indian Creek—can we then take credit for her better stories? I think not. Let those who are free of Texas enjoy their freedom. The books I am interested in investigating are native in the most obvious sense: set here, centered here, and, for the most part, written here. I see no point in going back beyond the thirties: anything earlier than that would be pioneer architecture—literary sod houses, so to speak. A few might be reasonably well-chinked, but the majority are as leaky as sieves, and about as uninteresting.

It is appropriate—indeed, inevitable—that a critique of Texas letters begin with the work of the Big Three: Roy Bedichek, W. P. Webb, and J. Frank Dobie. I wish it weren't inevitable—I had just as soon avoid it. The world outside never heard of Bedichek, hasn't read Webb, and isn't particularly interested in Dobie. The world inside doesn't read much and doesn't read well, but the three men were loved

and honored here. Their merits as men were long ago confused with their merits as writers, and quite understandably:
their merits as men were exceptional and easily perceived,
and few of the people who loved them had any skill in judging books. They were paid every homage but the homage of
acute attention. Such criticism as they got they probably got
from one another, for during the years of their prime there
was no reviewer in the state with either the guts or the
insight to say them nay.

Now they are dead. They have had a whole book of eulo-
gies* but no elegy, and something rather sad has happened.
Three men who disliked establishments have been made
into an Establishment, posthumously, and local belleletrists
are hard at work seeing that their memories are potted, pickled and preserved.

Not long ago I attended a meeting of the Texas Institute of
Letters, the first meeting I had been to since the deaths of
Dobie and Webb. During the afternoon there was a panel discussion, held in one of the grim ballrooms of the Driskill Hotel
in Austin. Our subject, equally grim, was "What Is The Texas
Institute of Letters?" A glance around the room would have
been sufficient to dispose of the question: we were a regional
writers' club. Some of us were a little less minor than others,
but none of us were causing any tremors in Stockholm. Only
the representative from Dallas, Mr. Lon Tinkle, took the question to heart; he suggested, not without eloquence, that we
should regard ourselves as a sort of Southwestern affiliate of
the Academie Francaise, a suggestion that drew sweet sighs
from his admirers and a muffled horselaugh or two from members less Gallic in spirit. As the afternoon inched toward its
close I noticed, over and over again, the name "Pancho" being

---

* *Three Men in Texas: Bedichek, Webb, and Dobie.* Ed. Ronnie Dugger.

tossed into conversations. Sometimes it had to be tossed a considerable distance. It was Mr. Dobie's nickname. Well, I thought, he was a very winning man; probably all these people were his friends. Mr. Bedichek and Dr. Webb came in for frequent and reverent mention too, but "Pancho" was a word the mere utterance of which conveyed a sort of literary status. By dinner time people were intoning it as if it were the password to heaven. Sanity seemed to be receding from the Driskill. The president-elect of the Institute introduced the dinner-speaker, Wallace Stegner, as if he were Shakespeare reincarnate, leaving Mr. Stegner numb with embarrassment at the podium. After the speech, prizes were doled out, the Trinity was invoked a few times for good measure, and the meeting closed. If I could have summoned one of the great Departed for the evening I would have summoned Mr. Bedichek. He wrote a good book on smells and could have fittingly described the odor of sycophancy that pervaded the Driskill that day.

༅

AFTER THE MEETING, IN PREPARATION for this book, I read the three men. That is, I read their books, twenty-nine in all. That I had not read them sooner is perhaps not as surprising as one would think. I grew up in a bookless town, in a bookless part of the state—when I stepped into a university library, at age eighteen, the whole of the world's literature lay before me unread, a country as vast, as promising, and, so far as I knew, as trackless as the West must have seemed to the first white men who looked upon it. It behooved me to locate Homer, Shakespeare, and the other major landmarks scattered through the stacks. My own backyard could wait.

I soon realized that some of the major landmarks were mountains I felt no desperate eagerness to climb, and in time I saw that the exploration of that country would be one of the day-to-day pleasures of a lifetime. I might have turned at that point to the immediate terrain, but for various reasons I did not. I wanted to be a novelist, not a naturalist, a historian, or a folklorist. Technical curiosity led me elsewhere, and for a time I looked upon the three men with that immodest disdain which young writers so frequently reserve for their better-established elders. Had I known the men personally I would probably have read them sooner, but unluckily I seem to have been the only writer in the state who did not know them personally. I saw Dobie twice, Webb twice, Bedichek not at all.

I knew, however, that I would have to read them someday. They were the Presences—only in exile could one ignore them. In twenty years this will change, and a generation that did not know them as men will be free to treat them as one treats most citizens of the republic of letters—that is, to decide from their books alone whether to admire them or dismiss them. Now it is not so simple. The writer my age who wishes to write about this state must relate himself one way or the other to the tradition they fostered, whether he reads the three men or not.

The twenty-nine volumes were long, the reckonings I make with them here very short. I distrust thumb-nail criticism but in this instance it is the only kind the context will admit. Perhaps it will do as a yard-stick, a means of measuring the distance from where Bedichek, Webb, and Dobie stood yesterday to where I and my colleagues stand today.

☙

BEDICHEK, THE WRITER, IS AS easy to like as Bedichek the man seems to have been. His achievement was modest and, in the best sense of the word, belleletristic. The pity is that he spent so much of his life doing essentially menial academic tasks and so little of it writing for publication. He was nearing seventy when he completed his first book, by which time his companions Dobie and Webb had each been writing for more than twenty years. Sentence by sentence Bedichek used language better than either of them, yet the weight of their lives lies directly behind their books, while the weight of Bedichek's lies somewhere to the side of his.

Of the three, he was the only one who could be counted a stylist. Webb's prose was utilitarian—careful, clear, and stiff in his early books, somewhat more supple in his last two. It could carry his dry, spare wit very well, but on the few occasions when he tried to make it carry his more poetic emotions the result was unlovely. Dobie's prose is strong and clear at times, and at other times makes one want to grind one's teeth. Bedichek had a fine ear and a style that is clear, firm, and graceful. His prose accomplishes the crucial task of slowing the reader down and putting him in rhythm with the subject, which is almost always Nature. He abhorred the hastiness of modern life, and a taste for the leisurely carried over into his prose. It slows the eye without slowing the mind. He demands that the reader take him at his own pace or not at all, and he enforces the demand the only way a writer can—with style.

A naturalist, of course, *must* have style these days if he hopes to be read by any but the specialists. Interest in Nature is declining, to say the least. Bedichek knew this and lamented it; Dobie and Webb knew it too, and they too lamented it. Indeed, the note of lamentation for Nature Despoiled is sounded so many times in the twenty-nine volumes that it comes near achieving the opposite of its intended effect. After a time one begins to wonder if man's divorce from Nature is really as bad and as belittling as they make it out to be.

Whether it is or no, we arrive immediately at the crucial difference between that generation of Southwestern writers and the generation that is developing now. Bedichek, Webb, Dobie and their disciples revered Nature, studied Nature, hued to Nature. At their worst they made a fetish of it; at their best they drew on it brilliantly for context and metaphor.

For my generation, the reverse holds—and will hold, I suspect, for the generations that follow. I doubt we could scrape up enough nature-lore between us to organize a decent picnic. To the Presences, that could only be a damning remark. For them, Nature was the Real. Knowledge of it made a full man, and accord with it was the first essential of the Good Life.

Well, to each his own. I spent more than twenty years in the country and I came away from it far from convinced that the country is a good place to form character, acquire fullness, or lead the Good Life. I have had fine moments of rapport with nature, but I have seen the time, also, when I would have traded a lot of sunsets for a few good books. Sentimentalists are still fond of saying that nature is the best teacher—I have known many Texans who felt that way, and most of them live and die in woeful ignorance. When I lived in the country I noticed no abundance of full men.

Of course one has to be careful not to mix terms, to confuse nature with country and country with anything which is not the city. One can love nature without loving the rural way of life, a distinction which both Bedichek and Dobie sometimes lost sight of. For better or worse, the country *has* been despoiled. Life in the country nowadays usually means life in or near the small town, and the small towns do not enlarge one's character, they shrink it.

On first reading, Bedichek appears to be one of those rare writers who can make the workings of nature interesting. A second reading corrects that impression: the appeal of his work is not informational at all. The appeal of his work is in the play of his mind. One does not read him to learn about the mocking bird, but to learn about Bedichek. Indeed, the more one reads him the less inclined one is to think of him as a naturalist. In his best essays he uses nature as a reference point from which to discourse generally upon life, and upon those things which most affect the quality of life, such as Time and Education. He was an old-style philosophic humanist whose formal affinities are with Emerson, Thoreau, and, very distantly, Montaigne. *Adventures With a Texas Naturalist* is the only one of his books one needs complete, but, oddly and unfortunately, some of his most trenchant and best informed writing is to be found in *Educational Competition* (1956), his history of the University Interscholastic League.

One is inclined to doubt that Bedichek would have claimed as much reading for himself as some of his friends have claimed for him. Like a sensible man, he read what interested him, and clearly not everything did. He shared with Dobie an aversion to twentieth century literature, though in both cases the grounds for the aversion are somewhat vaguely stated. Both seemed to feel that the literature of earlier centuries possessed a superior vitality, but neither apparently bothered to read enough modern literature to allow them to argue the point intelligently. Dobie in particular was given to reckless fulminations against the modern— some of his disciples have picked up the habit and will hardly trust themselves with anything later than Plato.

Bedichek's form, of course, was the reflective essay, but he also had something of the anatomist in him. His last book, *The Sense of Smell* (1960), is an anatomy. His theories on shitting, rumoured to be original, were unfortunately never committed to paper. Had he started writing earlier his sane, healthy eccentricities might have had more opportunity to manifest themselves—and Texas has long needed an eccentric with a good prose style.

🐝

IT HAS LONG NEEDED AN unsentimental historian, too, and came near to finding one in Walter Prescott Webb. The problem of sentiment has seldom been dealt with in discussions of the literature of this region, yet it is a central problem. Everyone who writes from Texas feels this to be his own, his native land, and no one yet has had a soul so dead that it would allow him to write about the state unsentimentally. In the majority of cases, however, it is less a question of live souls than of soft minds. The tough-minded Texan is a rarity, and the tough-minded Texas writer all but nonexistent. Webb observed as much himself, toward the end of *The Great Plains*: "There has been a tendency on the part of writers to mix a good deal of sentiment with their history of the West."* Yet a few years later, in his preface to *The Texas Rangers*, he could not resist contributing to the mixture:

> With assiduity I have sought out the veterans and heard their accounts. Men in active service have given me their *frijoles* and bread and black coffee. They have suffered me to share their camp, ride their best horses, fire their six-shooters, and to feel the companionship of men and horses when the saddle-stirrups touch in the solitudes . . .†

That is Webb being Dobie, or worse, Webb being a Texas Ranger. What a thrill it must have been for a humble professor, firing a Texas Ranger's six-shooter! Fortunately the passage is less typical of Webb than of Western sentiment gen-

---

* *The Great Plains*, p. 321.

† *The Texas Rangers*, Austin, 1966, xvi. I have not been entirely successful in purging my own pages of this sort of sentiment, a fact the censorious reader will doubtless note.

erally. In his time, Webb was the nearest thing to a tough-minded intellectual that the state had produced, and he was also the only thinker of any importance that it produced. The West has produced many good books, but perhaps, as yet, no great books. *The Great Frontier* may be the only book by a Texan that could with any accuracy be called major. Webb was shrewd enough to locate, while young, a crucial subject—the effect of the frontier on Western civilization—and he applied himself to it with the sort of tenacity which had probably enabled his forebears to survive on the hard soil of West Texas. Intellectual survival, in his time, took about as much stay-with-itness as physical survival had taken a generation earlier.

WEBB'S BOOKS VARY IN QUALITY, but they fit together in the way a writer's life-work ideally should. His work had scope, continuity, and coherence, and it can be seen, I think, that the farther his work took him from the borders of his native state the clearer and more effective he became and the safer he was from the blurring effects of sentiment.

The important books are *The Texas Rangers* (1935), *The Great Plains* (1931), *Divided We Stand* (1947) and *The Great Frontier* (1952). I list them in the order in which Webb conceived them; if they are read in that sequence one can follow the gradual expansion of his focus as he moved from local, to regional, national, and finally, international questions. Two of these, *The Texas Rangers* and *Divided We Stand,* seem to me to be of secondary merit, the one flawed by hero worship, the other no longer of much pertinence. The other two remain substantial complementary achievements.

The Texas Rangers is essentially his first book, though *The Great Plains* crowded ahead of it in order of publication. It is a flawed book, but by no means uninteresting. In criticizing it I should make clear that I am no student of Texas history and do not presume to dispute Webb's facts. The flaw in the book is a flaw of attitude. Webb admired the Rangers inordinately, and as a consequence the book mixes homage with history in a manner one can only think sloppy. His own facts about the Rangers contradict again and again his characterization of them as "quiet, deliberate, gentle" men.

In 1847, when the Rangers accompanied the United States Army into the City of Mexico, a sneak thief stole a handkerchief from them. They shot him. Another Mexican threw a stone and they shot him too. Later a Ranger named Allsens was killed in a violent district of the city and the Rangers shot eighty Mexicans in retaliation. Webb relates these facts without apparently considering that, while they might be the actions of men who were quiet and deliberate, they are hardly the actions of men who can accurately be called gentle.

His most glaring whitewash, however, occurs in the chapters in which he describes the career of Captain McNelly, a Ranger's Ranger and a man whom Webb seemed to admire above all others. In one of his least fortunate sentences he describes Captain McNelly's soul as a "flame of courage." Early in 1875 McNelly and his men were sent into the infamous Nueces Strip, that portion of Texas lying between the Nueces River and the Rio Grande. McNelly's job was to rid the area of cattle thieves, of which there were a great many. He did a brilliant, brave job, and his methods were absolutely ruthless. Any Mexican unlucky enough to be caught was tortured until he coughed up information, then summarily hung. Mexicans found with cattle were shot. In one of his boldest moves, McNelly and his thirty men crossed the Rio Grande to attack a ranch near Las Cuevas, where some 250 Mexican soldiers were assembled. Unfortunately the Rangers dashed into the wrong ranch and found a number of men working at the woodpile, cutting wood while their wives cooked breakfast. The Rangers shot them down, then realized their mistake and went on to the right ranch. Whether apologies were offered to the wives of the slain woodchoppers is not recorded. Webb is aware that McNelly's methods might conceivably be criticized, but he satisfies himself with the remark that "Affairs on the border cannot be judged by standards that hold elsewhere."*

Why they can't is a question apologists for the Rangers have yet to answer. Torture is torture, whether inflicted in Germany, Algiers, or along the Nueces Strip. The Rangers, of course, claimed that their end justified their means, but people who practice torture always claim that. Since the practical end, in this case, was the recovery of a few hundred cattle, one might dispute the claim. Only a generation or two earlier the Nueces Strip had been Mexico, and it is not inconceivable that some of the Mexicans involved had as good a right to the cattle as Captain Richard King or any other Texas cattleman. (Indeed, the Mexicans called them *nanitas'* cattle, grandmama's cattle.)

There are places, apparently, where the passage of a century changes very little, and the Texas border is such a place. One gains no popularity there today by suggesting that Mexicans have rights to something other than air, *frijoles,* and goat's milk. The farm-labor disputes of 1967—disputes in which the Texas Rangers played a suspect role—make this very clear. I know a farm manager, a man but recently migrated from the Valley to the High Plains, who was sincerely shocked by the fact that Mexicans were beginning to want houses to live in. Tents and truck-beds, fifty

---

* *The Texas Rangers,* p. 252.

cents an hour cash and a free goat every week or two no longer satisfied them. They had come to consider themselves human beings, an attitude which filled the manager with astonishment and vague dismay. When Mexicans become thus aberrated it is time, in Texas, to call in the Rangers.

ক্ষ্

WEBB WAS AWARE, OF COURSE, that the pacification of the border involved ethical questions that were a good deal more subtle than the Rangers' methods of resolution. The difficulty was that he simply could not bear to think badly of the Rangers. Even when he is forced to discuss the career of a Ranger who was an out-and-out bastard the worst he will say is that the man was not suited to Rangering and should not have been hired. In a book of almost six hundred pages he records virtually no instance in which a Ranger treats either a Mexican or a Negro as anything but a recognized inferior, and he seems to accept the still-common assumption that a Ranger can tell whether a Mexican is honest or dishonest simply by looking at him. The same method was used to separate good Negroes from bad. Captain Bill McDonald's famous advance on the Ft. Brown rioters in 1906, while no doubt a splendid example of Ranger courage, is an equally fine indication of their racial arrogance. McDonald, with one man, advanced on twenty armed men with these words:

> You niggers hold up there! I'm Captain McDonald . . . and I'm down here to investigate a foul murder you scoundrels have committed. I'll show you niggers something you've never been used to . . .*

---

* *The Texas Rangers*, p. 247.

The important point to be made about *The Texas Rangers* is that in it Webb was writing not as an historian of the frontier, but as a symbolic frontiersman. The tendency to practice symbolic frontiersmanship might almost be said to characterize the twentieth century Texan, whether he be an intellectual, a cowboy, a businessman, or a politician. One of the purposes of this book is to explore the ramifications of that tendency.

While it may be possible for a novelist to remain a symbolic frontiersman without impairing his art, the same will hardly hold for the historian. I think it is clear that most Southwestern writers sooner or later assume that role, and I am not sure that Webb ever quite developed beyond it. But he did, at least, have a firm commitment to intellect, and to intellectual process, which is more than can be said for most of his contemporaries. Indeed, it is more than can be said for either Bedichek or Dobie, both of whom displayed a marked ambivalence toward the intellect.

At the end of his career, in the final pages of *The Great Frontier*, Webb remarks briefly upon his own development:

> The first step in my preparation to become a student of the frontier was taken in 1892, when my parents moved to West Texas while that country was still in the frontier stage . . . all my early impressions were of young families struggling with raw nature. Thus it was that I touched the hem of the garment of the Great Frontier, almost but not quite too late. Because my father was a teacher, I had books and became a reader, and as I read I caught a distorted but alluring vision of another world . . . At an early age I determined to escape to that other world, and to leave the frontier to those who were more audacious . . . Eventually I turned to the frontier as a subject of study, and there I found a body of literature that I could under-

stand, and I found myself . . . And so I entered the door leading back to the world I had known.

Most of the writers who have come out of this region could make a similar statement. As late as the forties the hem of the garment of the Great Frontier could still be touched in rural Texas—perhaps there are a few places where it could be touched even now.

If I were recasting the statement to fit myself I would first of all change the figure and eliminate the word "hem." It suggests the feminine, and the frontier was not feminine, it was masculine. The Metropolis which has now engulfed it is feminine, though perhaps it is an error to sexualize the process even that much. The Metropolis swallowed the Frontier like a small snake swallows a large frog: slowly, not without strain, but inexorably. And if something of the Frontier remains alive in the innards of the Metropolis it is because the process of digestion has only just begun.

IN WRITING THIS CHAPTER I have begun to wonder if it is possible to write a discursive book about Texas which will not turn out to be simply a book for Texans, or, more narrowly still, a book for Texas intellectuals. One hopes not, but the doubt is not easily dispelled. In this age of information overload who but a few Texas writers could possibly need a critique of Roy Bedichek or J. Frank Dobie? The latter has had the largest audience of any Texas writer, but at that it is an audience composed primarily of middle-aged nostalgics, and it will probably not outlive him much more than a generation. The young writer who sets out to write about Texas will do well not to ask himself whom he is writing for: when one figures out the answer to that question the temptation is to quit wasting money on typewriter ribbons and to spend it instead on pipes and beer.

🐝

BEDICHEK'S BEST BOOK WAS HIS first, Webb's best book his last. Dobie's, in my opinion, came virtually without warning in 1935 and is called *Tongues of the Monte*. Oddly enough, for a man considered by his sponsors to be a sort of Tolstoy of the Texas soil, it is a book set entirely in Mexico. Texas is seldom mentioned, and Dobie is the only Texan who appears. It is a frankly fictionalized account of a year Dobie spent wandering in the mountains of Northern Mexico, a year he often described as the freest and happiest of his life. In his own bibliography of Southwestern literature, Dobie refers to the book twice, once under Mexico and once under Fiction:

> J. Frank Dobie is too fond of facts for a fictionist and too fond of stories for a historian. His *Tongues of the Monte* is a kind of fiction . . . woven almost entirely out of tales, characters, sayings, practices, and traditional lore of Mexico . . .*

One finds in Dobie and in Webb too a strong uncertainty about the imagination. Both revered it in other writers; neither was sure how far his own could be trusted. In their apprentice days they both attempted to write stories for the Western pulps, but the results were not encouraging and they gave up fiction for fact. The fundamentalist emphasis on literal truth may have had an inescapable hold on them, psychologically. Each occasionally casts a longing glance in

---

* *Guide to Life and Literature of the Southwest*, p. 100.

the direction of the novel, but only in *Tongues of the Monte,* when Dobie had crossed the Great River in fact and in symbol did one of them give his imagination a really free rein. The analogous book, for Webb, is of course *The Great Frontier,* in which he crosses the Atlantic and produces a dramatistic, if not a novelistic, history.

In truth, I think it may have been that Mr. Dobie was too fond of anecdotes to have made either a good novelist or a good historian. Except in his early books, the anecdote is his basic unit, a unit he grew more and more conditioned to by the weekly newspaper columns he produced without a miss for more than twenty years. At the end of his career he was virtually incapable of doing justice to any story that could not be told in three pages or less—doing justice to it in print, that is. From what one has heard he was a great raconteur. Unfortunately, great raconteurs who are also writers are all too often sloppy when they go to write down the stories they tell so well. At heart they are usually impatient with the written word and feel that it is a weak substitute for the human voice.* In their hands, it usually is. The labor of typing out a story that could be told effortlessly and pleasantly, in appreciative company, often wreaks havoc with their prose.

I think most readers who sit down and read Mr. Dobie's twenty-odd books will discover midway through *Coronado's Children* (his second) that he was just such a hasty and impatient writer. Despite his frequent, perhaps defensive, pronouncements about the noble prose of Malory, Montaigne, Dr. Johnson *et al.,* much of his own prose reads as if it had bored him to write it. I say that not to poor-mouth him, for I

---

* See *Some Part of Myself,* p. 271. The last sentence of Mr. Dobie's autobiography reads: "It's the despair of a writing man who has known the best of storytellers that he cannot translate their oral savor into print."

know that he worked in haste and had severe financial responsibilities to meet; nonetheless I think his prose reflects his own ambivalence toward literary activity. He seemed to have been plagued by a persistent sense that his books were a reduction of life, rather than an amplification of it. When he took over the editorship of the Publications of the Texas Folklore Society in 1923, it was left to him to write the notes on contributors, and he included one on himself:

> J. Frank Dobie, editor of the present volume, was born and reared on a ranch in the Texas border country, and although he is now an instructor in the University of Texas, he will always belong to the range.

He could never quite be comfortable with himself for having left the range, yet one suspects that at least as much of him belonged to the library. He left a superb personal library, including a range collection that was probably unexcelled, and despite his many reservations about the literary life, literature was his work. After *Tongues of the Monte,* my favorite of his books is the *Guide to Life and Literature of the Southwest* (1943). It is an excellent bibliography, and also essential Dobie: his terse, opinionated annotations make much better reading than the loose, poorly organized sequence of books on animals, though the latter got him much more acclaim.

He refused to copyright the *Guide.* The copyright page reads: "Anyone is welcome to help himself to any of it in any way." A few pages later, at the end of his introduction, he makes what for a bibliographer and scholar is a very curious apology:

> With something of an apologetic feeling I confess that I have read, in my way, most of these books. I should prob-

ably have been a wiser and better informed man had I spent more time out with the grasshoppers, horned toads and coyotes . . .*

Dobie never quite shook off the feeling that he ought to apologize for his book learning, a feeling one comes by naturally in the rural Southwest. Even today, in the country and the small towns, bookish interests are apt to be equated with deficient masculinity; but Dobie's ambivalence about the intellectual life relates not to this but to his feeling for nature. His brief remarks on nature in the *Guide* are repeated with slight variations many times in his books and essays:

> The ethnologists have taken Horse Culture, as well as themselves, very seriously. If there were time I would propound briefly and illustrate lengthily Coyote Culture, Rattlesnake Culture, Longhorn Culture, Roadrunner Culture . . . and several other cultures more delightful, sensible and profitable to a man with his roots deep in the soil of the Southwest than any form of culture derived from Italian operas, PhD theses on New England theology, and galleries of art devised to distort rather than illuminate life.

> Above all, consult the Grasshopper's Library. Listen to the owl's hoot for wisdom. Plant bean rows for peace . . . Studies are merely to "perfect nature." The only reality is nature itself.†

---

* *Guide*, p. 15.

† *Guide*, p. 84.

Feeling thus, it is doubtful that Dobie was ever entirely content with his vocation. For all his love of books he could never be quite sure that so much reading and writing did not constitute a betrayal of nature, or at the least, a divorce from her which might entail a loss of natural goodness and natural strength.

☙

DESPITE SUCH FEARS, HIS MOST useful work was often his scholarship. The animal books are, as I have said, repetitious, poorly organized, and, for the most part, dull. He relies heavily on paraphrase, but he never learned to paraphrase effectively. His biography of Ben Lilly,* on the other hand, is an excellent book on a man no one but Dobie could have got to; and the many introductions he contributed to reprints of Western texts are usually perceptive and helpful

His work with folklore is, I think, another matter. Dobie had perhaps too much personality to be a good collector, and in the long run it is his personality, not his knowledge of Southwestern folkways, that saves his books. The most serious objection that can be brought against his work in folklore is that, while he railed against prudery and expurgation, his own collecting was prudish and expurgated. One learns as little about the sexual mores of the cowboy from reading Dobie as one learns from the romantic Western fiction he so detested. Possibly his notebooks and letters, when published, will supply much that his books leave out, for he himself was well aware of the problem and mentions it in the introduction to his first book:

---

* *The Ben Lilly Legend*, Boston, p. 19.

Although there were cowboys mean, vicious, vulgar, dishonest, and cheap, even ignorant, they did not fit in; the general run of cowboys . . . could not be and were not ignorant or morally degraded. Yet, partly on account of the reasons that restrained Thackeray, a full delineation of the cowboy's masculinity, a quality interwoven with morality, is not in this book entered into . . . A frank and full—that is, a naturalistic—delineation of the cowboy as a man apart from his work and yet as a natural product of his own soil, remains to be done. It will probably be done only in fiction. Samuel Pepyses have been as rare in the West as in the East . . .*

Late in his life, when the reasons that restrained Thackeray must have seemed very remote, Dobie let a couple of well-salted anecdotes about Shanghai Pierce slip through into *Cow People*. Happily, he was never remiss in applauding others who were frank and full, for when Teddy Blue (a Pepys of a sort) published *We Pointed Them North* in 1939, Dobie was generous with his praise and quick to point out that one of the exceptional merits of that fine book is its honest treatment of the cowboy's relations with women.

🐚

TONGUES OF THE MONTE BELONGS to the literature of the marvelous journey. There is some folklore in it, but it is essentially a search for the real and the good. There are many echoes of its Cervantic model, the strongest being the character of the old guide, Inocencio, a slightly more wizened Sancho Panza. At the end the old man gives

---

* A *Vaquero of the Brush Country*, xii.

Dobie his knife, a fine blade which he calls "The Faithful Lover," and as they are waiting for the train that will take Dobie away Inocencio cuts a small vein in his wrist and with his own blood marks a cross in the palm of Dobie's hand:

"This sign is more than words," he said. "Soy el suyo. I am yours."

I stood on the rear platform of the lurching car until a curve cut off view of the station. As long as I looked I saw a little old man, who could be stately though, and who had muscles that never tired, an enormous straw hat on the ground beside him, making the gesture of the open heart toward me, touching his breast with the fingers of his hand and then extending his arms and holding them stretched out wide apart. I remembered a sentence from some writer of Mexico I had read: "Just as all plant life springs from the soil, so from it come also the souls of men."*

The South Texas that Dobie knew was dominated, then as now, by very ambitious men, and it is not surprising that he should have had to cross the Rio Grande to find his figure of innocence.

ॐ

I SAW MR. DOBIE ONLY twice, once at a literary party in Dallas in 1962, and the second time on a hot street in Austin only a month or two before he died. In Dallas he was a joy to watch, though in Dallas any happy man would be. It was

---

* *Tongues of the Monte*, p. 301.

February, but Dobie wore his white suit, and with that, his white hair and his roguish grin he seemed amid that somber, wintry company to project the combined appeal of Buffalo Bill and Dylan Thomas. In five minutes he had reduced the matrons to twinkles, giggles and coos.

In Austin, I was walking down Travis Street toward noon of a hot summer day, on my way to visit a bookshop, when I saw Mr. Dobie starting up the hill below me. He had a book in his hand and had probably just emerged from the shop I was meaning to visit. As he approached I debated speaking, but the day was broiling, I was carrying my young son, and Mr. Dobie was obviously concentrating on getting up the hill and into the shade. He didn't look up and I said nothing, but when I crossed the street at the foot of the hill I saw him at the top, his Stetson pushed back and his white hair fallen on his brow, resting a moment by a parking meter. Though I did not know him and at that time did not care for his books I felt that catch in the heart that always comes when I see that one of the Old Ones of this land will soon be gone, no more to ride the river nor follow the Longhorn cow.

❧

BENICHEK, WEBB, AND DOBIE; AND who else? Are there perhaps neglected classics gathering dust in the Southwestern sections of our libraries? I think not. The most impressive Texas book of the thirties is J. Evetts Haley's superb biography of Goodnight.* Haley is a well-educated, disciplined historian; he wrote better prose than either Webb or Dobie and it is a pity he has contracted so virulent a conservatism. In recent years he has become the Captain Queeg of Texas letters.

---

* *Charles Goodnight: Cowman and Plainsman*, Boston, 1936.

No fiction of interest was produced in Texas before the fifties. Some have tried to make a case for George Sessions Perry, whose contribution boils down to one honest but flat depression novel (*Hold Autumn in Your Hand*, 1941) and one slight piece of engaging schmaltz (*Walls Rise Up*, 1939). The books by Texans that began to appear in the fifties wore a very different stamp from those that had appeared in the thirties and forties. They wore the stamp of the modern—derivative modern, in most cases, but modern nonetheless. One began to meet epigraphs from Rimbaud (William Goyen's *The House of Breath*) and Faulknerian complexity (William Humphrey's *Home from the Hill*). What is more important, the balance suddenly shifts from the discursive to the imaginative, from history and quasi-history to fiction and poetry.

It is not that the frontier ethos had inhibited reflection: Dobie, Webb, and Bedichek were all reflective men. What it apparently inhibited was the more introspective modes of expression. One may write, on the frontier, but one must write about the world that is or was, not about the person one is or the world one might imagine. It may be that World War II had a part in destroying that check, for the generation that developed in its aftermath were committed from the first to introspection, and to a conscious search for models and methods. It was not until the war, apparently, that Texas writers learned they could leave the state without turning to dust at the borders. Dobie and Webb had spent time in England, it is true, but one gets the impression that neither of them were ever really at home northeast of Austin. Humphrey, Goyen, John Graves, John Howard Griffin are all as at home in Europe as they are in Texas.

The war and the change of scene seems also to have freed our writers from the frontier conviction that existence is justified only by incessant work. The Texas writers of the fifties are a quiet, unostentatious bunch, and the best of their books, *The Ordways*, *Goodbye to a River*, Vassar Miller's *Adam's Footprint*, are the products of imaginations working leisurely, in neither fury nor haste. In that respect they throw back to Bedichek.

🍃

NOWADAYS, OF COURSE, TEXAS WRITERS are scattered high, wide and lonesome. The generation of which I am a member has barely got started, yet already a younger generation blossoms beneath our feet. A hastily constructed literary map of the state shows that novelists in veritable swarms have begun to emerge from the small towns. One notes the (to me) extraordinary fact that such communities as Chillicothe, Archer City, Stamford, Clarksville, Floydada, Groesbeck, Alvarado, Abilene, and Dundee have produced novelists and can thus no longer be considered intellectually virgin. Some, of course, probably consider that they have been intellectually raped; but if we assume, as we must, that the writers who have published are merely the top of the iceberg (or let's say the ant-bed), the prospect is little short of terrifying. If these creative writing courses aren't stopped, every town in Texas will have its novelist within a decade, and the novelists will have to follow the lead of the oilman and apply for a depletion allowance.

It is sometimes tempting to sit back and take a Maileresque glance at the talent in the room, but the minute one draws up a list the temptation diminishes. Such a list would include Humphrey, Goyen, Graves, Griffin, Vassar Miller, R. G. Vliet, Donald Barthelme, Terry Southern, John Rechy, Aubrey Goodman, Bill Brammer, Walter Clemons, Elroy Bode, June Arnold, Sherry Kafka, Robert Flynn, Mack Thomas, Edwin Shrake, the Texas Observers—who all and wherever they are, or let's say Willie Morris, Ronnie Dugger, and Larry King—Al

Dewlen, William Harrison, Hughes Rudd, Dorothy Yates, Grover Lewis, Tom Horn, Max Crawford, Dave Hickey, and a number of others whose light can be counted on to burst upon the world almost any time. There might be a major talent lurking in that thicket of names, but if so I am not the one to scare it out. I only hope that a desire to escape the Johnsonian taint doesn't drive too many of the younger writers out of the state before they have had time to become well-seeded with local experience. Texas writers are sometimes so anxious to avoid the accusation of provincialism that they will hardly condescend to render the particularities of their own place, though it ought to be clear that literature thrives on particulars.

The material is here, and it has barely been touched. If this is truly the era of the Absurd, then all the better for the Texas writer, for where else except California can one find a richer mixture of absurdities? Literature has coped fairly well with the physical circumstances of life in Texas, but our emotional experience remains largely unexplored, and therein lie the dramas, poems, and novels.

An ideal place to start, it seems to me, is with the relations of the sexes, a subject from which the eyes of Texas have remained too long averted. There are those who feel that I have dealt with the subject exhaustively in my three novels, an opinion that speaks poorly for some people's knowledge of life. In the section which follows I would like to deal with the subject again.

Eros in Archer County

SEX IS STILL a word to freeze the average Texan's liver, particularly if the Texan is over forty and his liver not already pickled. The young toss the word around carelessly, but adults do not, for careless use might implicate them in suspect acts or suspect attitudes. The young, of course, are mostly urban now, and they seem to be adapting themselves handily to the promiscuity of the age.

At the moment, however, I am not interested in describing or evaluating the sexual attitudes that prevail in present-day Texas. That pleasant task can be better taken up in the novel. What urgently needs to be done is to get down what can still be remembered of the sexual attitudes that prevailed here in the recent and not-so-recent past. As Dobie rightly observed, the frontier produced no Pepys. Teddy Blue was frank and funny, but all too succinct. The few pages he devotes to the traildrivers' activities with women are the nearest thing to sexual autobiography that we have for the nineteenth century West, and that we have no more should hardly occasion surprise. There were the reasons that restrained Thackeray, the verbal inhibition that even to this day has lost but little of its power in the rural West. Besides, the nineteenth century West was without a leisure class, and that made a great difference in its literary production. The novels of Henry James and the fantasies of *My Secret Life* were alike impossible to it. Life in the West was itself such a strenuous physical adventure that the need for psychic or sexual adventure may have been diminished. Had the author of *My Secret Life* lived in the West he would have gone raving mad with frustration. There just weren't that many women west of the Mississippi, and what there were tended to be rather work-worn, and a discouraging distance apart.

FORTUNATELY FOR THE INVESTIGATOR, I think one can assume a certain consistency of attitude in the West from about the time of the Civil War until at least World War I. Those of us whose parents were born in the first decade of this century and whose grandparents were born in the sixties and seventies of the last century have usually had abundant opportunity for contact with a nineteenth century sexual orientation. For the novelist, the principal difficulty is one of language, since the novelist needs not merely knowledge of attitudes but knowledge of the language and, indeed, the tones in which the attitudes are expressed. It is the private speech of one's grandparents and their contemporaries that one would have liked to have heard—what they said to one another in the morning in the kitchen or at night in the bedroom, if indeed they bothered to speak in either place. Without the language and the tones of the private moment it is impossible to re-create in fiction the emotional realities of the lives one's forebears lived. The novelists who have attempted to write about the nineteenth century West have one and all come up against this problem of speech, and they have one and all been weakened by it. Their dialogue is usually an unconvincing mixture of the contemporary and the archaic, bad enough when they have two men talking but really hopeless when they try to render the conversation of men and women. It is this inadequacy of dialogue that makes so much of the fiction of the West seem stilted and not quite believable, even when written by novelists who are competent otherwise.

While it is unfortunate that we know so little about what people thought, felt and said about their bodies and their sexual activities in pioneer Texas, what is really sobering is to reflect that unless someone gets busy we will have recorded little more of what they thought, felt and said about those matters in the thirties and forties. The reasons that restrained Thackeray and Mr. Dobie also restrained virtually everyone who wrote about the Southwest prior to the fifties. It was impossible to write frankly about sexual matters—even in a discursive book—without bringing upon oneself the opprobrium of elderly ladies, to whose opinions the pillars of our communities and a great many of our writers have always deferred.

There seems now little reason to allow these well-meaning ladies to be a deterrent to frankness, and I should like to set down, ere memory fades, a few not-quite-random notes on the sexuality of small town Texas, as I remember it from the forties and early fifties. The reader will keep in mind that when I titled this chapter I did not claim much in the way of territory: just Archer County. I was something of a stay-at-home in my youth and can't vouch for what went on down in Jack County, much less for remote areas like Ft. Worth and Dallas. Indeed, I'm not even sure that my observations in Archer County were really thorough, but I'm afraid they will have to suffice. The chances of anyone volunteering to fill me in on what I may have missed are now lamentably slim.

❦

MY OWN FIRST BRUSH WITH small-town restrictions on frankness followed almost immediately upon the realization that sex was something worth being frank about. I was eight or nine years old, as I recall, and was climbing a street-sign pole. When I started up the pole I had no purpose in mind but casual exercise, but about the time I got to the top, the flexing activity that pole-climbing involves produced what I learned years later was an orgasm. I had not been expecting anything so delightful to happen at the top of that pole, and I hung for a moment in amazement before sliding down. A lady of my acquaintance happened to be standing nearby, so I hurried over and gave her an ecstatic report on the event. My description was probably rather vague, but I was able to pinpoint the area that felt so good, and that was enough for the lady. "Ssh," she said, looking apprehensively about. "Just don't tell anybody."

❦

BUT I DID TELL, OF course, and so did my young companions. Where the young were concerned, the verbal restrictions were extremely ineffective; or were, at any rate, for a period of years. Curiously enough, among the youth of my hometown, the prepubertal years were the period of greatest verbal license. First graders, for the most part, were a sheltered and inarticulate lot, but by the time one reached the second grade one's vocabulary was swollen with forbidden words picked up on the farm-yard, in the schoolbus, or on the playground.

We knew, of course, that such words were rightly the property of adults, and we were careful to use them only among ourselves. Careless use at home would have meant nothing less than the chain-and-block, and very few of us ever slipped up. "Shit," "piss," "fuck" and "goddamn" were in extremely common use among second and third graders during the early forties, and little girls used them almost as readily as little boys. At that time the one innocent word in the group was "fuck." Toilet-training had already placed a strong inhibition on reference to the excretory functions, and most of us had been to Sunday school often enough to realize that we could not expect to go to heaven if we took the Lord's name in vain. The God most of us envisioned was definitely of a prohibitive bent, and was known to have the power to enforce His demands. We were a good deal more afraid of Him than we were of our early earthly parents; only the more heathen among us could say "goddamn" without sooner or later glancing nervously at the sky.

"Shit" and "piss" we used with less hesitation. So far as we knew, they were not particularly offensive to God, and by that time it was a relief to escape the forest of euphemisms that had grown up around the waste products. Visits to one's friends were apt to be a bit chancy, since each household had its own set of permissible euphemisms. Some of the more enlightened (and antiseptic) families utilized the time-honored mathematical formula of Number One and Number Two, but these were in the minority. Others preferred the onomatopoetic "tinkle" for pissing; a few admitted "weewee," but "pee" and "peepee" were looked upon with disfavor, no doubt because they suggested that the penis was involved. "Pot" was standard for shitting; "do-do" was considered affected. A few preferred the evocative "grunt," while others adopted an alphabetical code and said

Big T and Little T. The safest approach of all was simply to ask for the bathroom, leaving one's hostess in comfortable doubt as to the activity to be pursued therein.

Bathrooms, incidentally, were seldom lockable. The young were known to be given to masturbation, a practice lockable doors would surely encourage. Not even surveillance could eliminate it entirely, but it did render it respectably nerve-wracking.

Probably the little girls used profanity because it seemed to offer an entree into the boy's world; it took no great intelligence to perceive that in that part of the country the boy's world was the more desirable one. As puberty approached, all but a few diehard tomboys gave up and resigned themselves to being women, and for the next few years unchaste expressions seldom crossed their lips. If a girl were especially vexed she might use "shit" as an exclamation, but only if she were in the company of people by whom she wished to be thought daring. Coarse language became the recognized prerogative of males, and they guarded it zealously.

To second and third graders, as I have said, "fuck" was an innocent word. Few of us had any clear idea what it meant, and we ordinarily used it in its adjectival form. In retrospect, I realize that one of the more stunning verbal slips I ever heard was made by a nine-year-old chum who at the Sunday dinner table asked his sister to pass the fucking butter. The adults were too stunned for effective response, and we children merely giggled, not realizing that the word was all that bad.

At that tender age we seldom used, or needed to use, the vernacular words for the genital organs. Of those, the one subject to the severest prohibition was the word "cunt," and I think the prejudice against it was a class prejudice. It was unknown to us as children, adolescents used it very rarely, and the only time I can recall hearing adults use it was when I was in the camp of some semi-civilized laborers who made their living grubbing mesquite and piling prickly pear, a family so low on the ladder of class that they shared their camp with Mexicans.

In Texas the word was partially rehabilitated by the college youth of the fifties, but its use here is still rather guarded. During the filming of *Hud* several prominent citizens of the Panhandle were dismayed to learn that among Californians it occurs quite frequently in light conversation.

"Cock" was in fairly common use in the forties, but the most popular word for the penis was "dick." "Cock" was most frequently heard in "cocksucker"; the wide use of the latter as a term of derogation would seem to speak eloquently enough of the area's strong heterosexual bias, but in fact the term "cocksucker" was used in ways which suggest some ambivalence. "Prick" was frequently used as a term of insult, whereas "cocksucker" was more often used joshingly, in moments of high locker-room camaraderie. At such times it came nearer to being a term of affection or comradeship, not an accusation of perversion. Of course there were times when it was used as an insult, usually about ten seconds before a fight broke out, but I never heard anyone seriously accuse a person of performing the act which the word suggests. There was, I believe, a tacit understanding that only one's friends could call one a cocksucker without expecting retaliation.

Of course the Code of the West carried with it an extremely strong prohibition against overtly homosexual action—so strong indeed that most of us did not really believe in homosexuality as a physical possibility until we reached college age. I witnessed a good deal of youthful homoerotic exhibitionism, but nothing more clear cut than that, and I can recall only two occasions on which there was group masturbation, both on afternoons when it was too hot to play baseball.

A charge of homosexuality, directly leveled, would have produced a fight instantly. "Eat my dick" was an unignorable insult and always meant a fight, whereas "go fuck yourself" was a phrase that one was free to take or leave. It was flung about so frequently that it soon lost most of its force. "Motherfucker" was in the same category—it was generally bestowed good-humouredly. Few considered incest a real possibility, except perhaps between siblings. Very few of my middle-class companions had siblings who could be induced to experiment with them sexually, but there were always one or two lower-class families on the literal (and psychological) edge of the community where such experimentation was less dangerous and more frequent.

✍

BEFORE LEAVING EROTIC VOCABULARY TO discuss other forms of erotic behaviour I should like to consider what seems to me a dominant characteristic of the sexual life of West Texas, and this is the widespread tendency to confuse the genital with the anal. *Inter urinas et faeces nascimur,* and the general feeling seems to have been that one could never afterward venture into that place without risking a physical and possibly a moral befoulment. Mention sex in West Texas and someone will be sure to say, "I'm not going to talk about that crap." By far the commonest local response to my three novels has been: "Well, I liked the story but I wish you'd left out that other crap," the other crap being presumably the sexual description.

Sex is clearly and frequently equated with the waste products, and energy given to sex is thought to be energy wasted. Those who appear to believe that sexual fulfillment is more important than material success are generally referred to as "trashy people," and books about such people are said to be "trashy books." The most widely used terms of contempt are terms which combine an anal product with a suggestion of animality (horse's ass, chicken-shit), though of course the less eloquent dispense with even this subtlety and simply say "you asshole" or "you turd."

Scatology is also widely used as a method of sexual intimidation. In its crude form this generally involves the stupid flinging shit at the smart, for in the small town the person with brains poses a direct threat to the masculinity (or femininity) of the person without them. Many a smart kid had his face pushed into a commode bowl at one time or another, and not a few have endured analgesic enemas and other rectal horrors. I have a bright friend who grew up in a rural area when outhouses were still in use; by the time he reached the second grade his intelligence had marked him as dangerous and on days when he had the temerity to answer questions in class he would be ganged up on at recess and shoved through one of the holes in the men's outhouse, down into the shit. He was a senior in college when I met him, but he still showed a marked reluctance to answer questions in class.

The type of scatological put-down which President Johnson is said to employ from time to time in his dealings with Kennedy-ites, Ivy Leaguers, and his opponents in the Congress may well have been learned in the Hill Country schoolyards of his youth. I myself once knew a basketball coach who dressed down his players while sitting on the commode.

❦

THERE ARE, HOWEVER, MORE SUBTLE and more damaging aspects of the anal-genital confusion. In the late forties and early fifties adults still felt it incumbent upon them to stifle adolescent sexuality if at all possible, and a basic element in their strategy was to equate sex with shit, physical love with filth. Masturbation was filthy, and copulation, a process known to involve not one but two sets of human genitals, could only be filthier still. One might catch a repulsive disease, or produce a repulsive baby whose life would inevitably be dark and squalid.

Fortunately, most of us were not overly fastidious as adolescents and managed to make some sexual progress despite the constant danger of contamination. Some progress, but not much. For the boys, losing one's virginity was an initiatory event, important but not especially pleasurable. Most of the boys in my hometown had accomplished it by the age of fourteen, 99% of them with the same accommodating girl. After the initiation had been undergone, most of us, convinced we had syphilis at the least, went home determined to rot quietly away, and while waiting for the fevers and the fits we fell victim to the second element of the adult's strategy: athleticism.

High school athletics were not easily seen through. When kept in perspective, of course, there is no reason to see through them: sport is sport, and lots of fun, and there is nothing particularly bad about separating boys and girls in the afternoon and organizing them into teams and seeing to it that they burn off their surplus energies chasing one ball after another. Unfortunately, in most small towns, the perspective soon slips. The adults of the town, and particularly the men, tend to participate vicariously and over-zealously in high school athletics, and to make them, in a sense, a form of sexual compensation. Their compensation. This in time has its effect on the boys, for it is repeatedly made clear to them that the adults regard them as approvably and sufficiently masculine in proportion to how good they are at chasing the balls. Football is the glory sport. As practiced in the small town, it tends to point the male directly away from the female, toward the company of his athletic peers. The female is excluded, and further demeaned by being thrown a sop (cheerleading) in which her only function is to applaud the prowess of the male. The most applaudable, of course, is the quarterback, despite the fact that he regularly hunches up behind the center in a somewhat sodomitic pose. Football is the manliest of sports, and better a little symbolic sodomy than a lot of irresponsible fucking.

If I exaggerate the extent to which the youth of the small towns were suckered with athletics, I exaggerate only a little. Most of my small-town contemporaries spent their high school years trying desperately to be good athletes, because the attitude of the adults had them quite convinced that their sexual identity depended upon their athletic performance. Some of them shed this conviction rather quickly, once they were out of school, but others of them have not shed it yet, and never will.

Once in a while, of course, things turn out well. A few years ago our local eleven won the state One-A Championship, and the enraptured citizenry bought a commemorative cannon and set it on the courthouse lawn, a proud reminder, and probably the nearest thing to a penis ever to be exhibited in those parts.

❦

DESPITE THE ARGUMENT FROM FILTH and the pressures of athleticism, the adults of the town were not really successful in their attempts to stifle adolescent sexuality. The best they could manage, and that with the help of religion, was to make us feel guilty about the whole business. The guilt didn't stop anyone, it just cut into the pleasure. Ironically, what really defeated the adults was their own social symbology, in which, at this time, the automobile was extremely important. All possible means might be used to deprive teen-agers of sex, but it would have been a sin against class to deprive them of cars, and of course when they gave us cars they gave us the means to escape the sexual prohibition. As soon as we got cars we could join in the great Saturday night sport of pussy-hunting, foraging as far afield as Olney, Holiday, and Wichita Falls. The area was heavily hunted, of course, and we seldom ran much to ground, but we had lots of fun and learned a few things in the pursuit.

༖

WHEN DESPERATE, THERE WERE ALWAYS animals. I have written elsewhere about this aspect of smalltown sexuality, but since that text is somewhat obscure perhaps I can be forgiven for quoting the relevant passage here:

"We could go down to the stockpens," Leroy suggested. "There's a blind heifer down there we could fuck . . . There's enough of us we could hold her down."

The prospect of copulation with a blind heifer excited the younger boys almost to frenzy, but Duane and Sonny, being seniors, gave only tacit approval. They regarded such goings-on without distaste, but were no longer as rabid about animals as they had been. Sensible youths, growing up in Thalia, soon learned to make do with what there was, and in the course of their adolescence both boys had frequently had recourse to bovine outlets. At that they were considered overfastidious by the farm youth of the area, who thought only dandies restricted themselves to cows and heifers. The farm kids did it with cows, mares, sheep, dogs, and whatever else they could catch. There were reports that a boy from

90

Scotland did it with domesticated geese, but no one had ever actually witnessed it. It was common knowledge that the reason boys from the dairy farming communities were reluctant to come out for football was because it put them home too late for milking and caused them to miss regular connection with their milk cows.

Many of the town kids were also versatile and resourceful—the only difficulty was that they had access to a smaller and less varied animal population. Even so, one spindly sophomore whose father sold insurance had once been surprised in ecstatic union with a roan cocker spaniel, and a degraded youth from the north side of town got so desperate one day that he crawled into a neighbor's pig pen in broad daylight and did it with a sow.

"I say a blind heifer beats nothing," Leroy said, and no one actively disagreed with the sentiment . . .*

When the book was published the passage involving the blind heifer was apparently regarded as hyperbole, another of my many unkind cuts against my hometown. It was, however, sober realism. Masturbation excluded, bestiality was the commonest and by far the safest method of obtaining sexual release available to adolescent boys in those days. Indeed, if adults were tolerant of anything sexual, they were tolerant of bestiality—or at least passive toward it. Less onus attached to it than to masturbation, I would say. Incredible though it seems, the belief that masturbation led to blindness and insanity had not quite died out by the forties, and the campaign against the solitary vice was constant and vigorous.† Animals, on the other hand, were exempt from the protection of God and man, and, for all concerned, a big

---

* *The Last Picture Show*, p. 84.

† I won't quote, but see *The Last Picture Show*, Chapter XX.

mark in their favor was that they could not be impregnated. That, come to think of it, was the *only* mark in their favor.

❧

THE ORIGINS OF THE ANAL-GENITAL confusion are not too difficult to understand. That the region would tend to produce a predominantly anal orientation is quite natural: it was by all accounts a hard region to settle, and only people with a strong retentive capacity could have hung on there and survived. An emphasis on accumulation was also natural, for the area originally gave very little in the way of natural provender. The summer was a time of almost frantic storing: vegetables were canned, fruits preserved and, when cool weather came, pigs and beeves killed and hung up in the smoke house. We never thought of Mother Nature as a fruitful female who was generous with Herself; what one got from Her one earned. From nature one got no sense of sex as gift, much less a sense that sex was something in which both partners could delight. If one observed cattle, horses, sheep, dogs, or chickens one got the sense that sex was something aggressive males forced upon more or less reluctant females.

That is, of course, the view of sex our parents held, or held, at least, when they were young. One assumes it was the view our grandparents held, but about all we know about the sexual beliefs of our grandparents is what little can be deduced from the size of their families. Unfortunately, the fact that most of them had large families tells us little about their sex lives. Procreation had a clear social value on the frontier, for strength lay in numbers and children were needed to help with the work. Contraception was primitive or nonexistent, there were no media distractions, and the church-house was thirty miles away in the nearest town. If women thought of themselves in terms of a sexual role the role was clearly motherhood, and in one's children came one's pleasure and fulfillment. Sex itself was a privilege for the male, a duty for the female. It is hard indeed to think where the pioneer woman would have picked up such a sophisticated notion as that of a sexual role, and, isolated and overworked as she was, it is even harder to see what good it would have done her if she had picked it up.

❦

YEARS AGO SOMEONE POINTED OUT that Texas is hell on women and horses. He was wrong about horses, for most horses are considered to be valuable, and are treated well. He was absolutely right about women, though: the country was simply hell on them, and remained so until fairly recently. The pioneer woman had to cope with deprivation and physical hardship, but I am not sure but what the women who came to maturity in Texas in the twenties and thirties were even worse off. They had to cope, not with raw nature, but with a new and difficult concept of womanhood, one for which nothing in their early training had prepared them. They suddenly found themselves expected to be the equals of men, not merely socially and politically, but sexually as well. For a girl whose mother had been a pioneer, that leap would almost always be too great, particularly since in most cases she would by this time have moved to one or another of the small towns and fallen under the sexually crippling influence of small-town fundamentalism. The same saddening story filters down to one from the sons and daughters of women who are now in late middle age: they got along okay with their husbands until they learned they were supposed to have orgasms too, after which there was generally confusion and distress. How is the female to switch in one generation from an orientation which sees the act of love as a duty to one which sees it as a pleasure? It cannot easily be done, and perhaps it cannot be done at all unless the woman has a husband who is sensitive to her. Most West Texas husbands of that generation were notably insensitive to their wives, and I find it difficult to believe that very many of them even wanted to understand their wives' sexual dilemma. Understanding would have increased responsibility and most of them seemed to feel themselves heavily enough burdened with female demands as it was. As the women learned that they were supposed to have sexual privileges too the domestic life of the town became more and more uneasy. A sexual separatism developed, with the men hanging out with the men (at ballgames, birdhunts, etc.) and the women hanging out with the women (at socials, bridge parties, and church activities). At times in the forties one might have got the impression that men and women alike were basically homosexual, but that was hardly the case. They were mutually frightened and inhibited, and suffered the emotional crises that people probably always suffer in periods of rapid transition. Men who were quite content with the nineteenth century were suddenly having to cope with women who had begun to take an interest in the twentieth, and the coping wasn't simple.

Then, in the forties, came affluence. Money. It was not the solution to what ailed them, but to men and women who had been poor all their lives it offered a novel escape. Until the forties, a great many Texans *had* been poor all their lives, and when they began to come into the money it was natural that they should overrate it and expect the wrong things of it. They had imagined it would make them happier with one another, and they resented one another all the more when it didn't. Men made money and women spent it. If one spent unstintingly, sexual poverty might be disguised. Spending might accomplish what fucking hadn't, especially if one went at the spending regularly and passionately. New houses, new cars, new clothes, wall-to-wall carpets and wall-to-wall bric-a-brac, gadgets and appliances, living room sets so uniformly ghastly one would have liked to burn the factory that made them, these were the order of the day in the forties.

The affluence reached far down into the middle class, where most of us were growing up, but perhaps its most interesting effects were to be observed not among the many who were beginning to be reasonably prosperous but among the comparative few who, in a few short years, got unreasonably rich. Most of these got rich in oil, or in businesses related to oil. You do not, in a few short years, get rich in cattle; and indeed by this time it was already too late to get rich in cattle, no matter how many years you had.

Before the forties were over we had with us those new bulwarks of Southwestern masculinity, the millionaires— our world-famous *nouveax riches*. The world thought they were pretty funny, too, as they went about waving tokens of munificence and seeking desperately for the one great Purchase that would establish their value in the eyes of all. The joke turned sour only recently, when one of them got to be President.

The era of the Big Spenders is now almost over here, and were it not that Mr. Johnson's behaviour so continually calls it to mind, one would probably be inclined to treat the *nouveau* of the forties and fifties rather sentimentally, as one treats a vanishing breed. Amid the bland Texas middle class, our vulgar rich can seem baroque and delightful, and indeed, certain of them *are* delightful. As a class, however, they exhibit all the difficulties of the desperately confused, and they are dangerous in proportion to the amount of power they wield. They are frequently very able and very strong people, but I have yet to meet one whose abilities or whose strength counterbalances his insecurity. To reassure themselves, they brag and deal and buy, but the nerve of self-doubt remains always exposed and the slightest pressure on it can bring them near to panic. They will do anything to win love, but they usually fail at it because their fear of opening themselves is stronger than their desire to be loved. Whenever possible, they open their wallets instead, and most of them end by subsuming all relationships into one: the relation of owner to owned. What cannot be owned they destroy or ignore.

Like LBJ, they are most of them pseudo-ranchers. In Texas a ranch is the equivalent of a distinguished geneology—it establishes one's connection with the past. Here it is better to be a drugstore cowboy than no cowboy at all. Even the rich, who don't take money lightly, know that it is a lighter thing than land, and many a wealthy veteran of the oil-patch has smoothed over his most basic doubts about his own value by buying a valuable piece of land and putting a few toy cattle on it.

❧

OF COURSE THE SEPARATISM WHICH one saw in the small town in the forties had existed on the frontier, but then it was a separatism based upon work. Men's work took them away from women, and most of them were content with that arrangement. Anyone who has spent much time with cowboys will have observed that cowboys are a good deal more comfortable with one another than they ever are with their women, but I think it would be facile to assume from this that most cowboys are repressed homosexuals. Most cowboys are repressed heterosexuals. The tradition of the shy cowboy who is more comfortable with his horse or with his comrades than with his women is certainly not bogus. Cowboys express themselves most naturally, and indeed, most beautifully, through their work; when horseback they perform many extraordinarily difficult acts with ease and precision and grace. As the years pass they form very deep bonds with the men (and the horses) they work with, but I think the reason these friendships (mateships, the Australians call them) are so relaxed and so lasting is because they are nonsexual and offer a relief from the sexual tensions of the household. The cowboy's work is at once his escape and his fulfillment, and what he often seeks to escape from is the mysterious female principle, a force at once frightening and attractive.

The basic difficulty, I think, is that the cowboy lacks a style that would put him at ease with women and women at ease with him. His code has prepared him to think of women not as they are, nor even as they were, but in terms of a vague nineteenth century idealization to which not even the most proper plainswoman could really conform. The discrepancy between what the cowboy expected of women and what they needed of him accounts for a lot of those long rides into the sunset, as the drifting cowboy drifts away not so much from what he might want as from what he is not sure how to get. Women shook his confidence because it was a confidence based on knowing how to behave in a man's world, and even the West isn't entirely a man's world anymore.

༒

AMID SUCH TENSIONS, MY GENERATION grew up. If we escaped permanent imprisonment in an obsolete sexual orientation, we escaped it by the skin of our teeth; and I think much of the credit for that escape must go to the movies, or, at least, to the media. Where else were we to get ideas about sex that had as much force as the ideas that were pressed on us at home and in church? In movies we saw women kissing back and realized early that the female might be responsive rather than reluctant. The images we saw may have left us slightly more visually oriented than is good, but they convinced us, at least, that sex was not necessarily something to be frightened of, and that was more than we could have learned at home.

Though it seems incredible, we probably derived a more realistic view of women from the movies than we got from our homelife and our social experience. This may of course be a chicken-or-the-egg sort of argument, for no doubt movies were changing women as rapidly as they were changing our ideas about them. At any rate, they gave us images and examples to set against the repressive dicta we all inherited.

But, as I said earlier, I do not want to write about "us" as adults here. Our encounters with and part in the sexual revolution of the fifties and sixties, our proclivities for bohemianism, adultery, divorce and other once-undreamt-of novelties, these must await another occasion. It is time now to have a look at the landscape. It may lack the piquancy of our sexual customs, but, as many a traveler can attest, there is a great deal of it to be looked at.

A Look at the Lost Frontier

READERS OF *HOWARD'S END* will recall that Margaret Schlegel, at the age of twenty-nine, longed to see life steadily and see it whole. When I was twenty-nine I had the same ambition in regard to Texas. Or, at least, I feigned such an ambition in order to weasel a little traveling money out of a magazine. There are times when one just feels like driving.

By that time I had written three novels about Texas without bothering to travel much in it, and it seemed to me I ought to get out and store up a few new perceptions. I was willing to perceive anything that lay reasonably close to the road. Early one warm, foggy November morning I left my home in Houston and headed south, toward Mexico. I had decided to drive first to Brownsville, in the far southeastern tip of the state; then I would turn north and drive for days and days until I eventually came to Texline, in the far northwestern corner. Such a route would expose me to almost fifteen hundred miles of Texas—enough, perhaps, to give me some inkling of what the state looked like.

As I left Houston the lights from the many motels colored

the fog orange and green, like the fogs in cheap science-fiction movies. One sometimes wonders if Bowie and Travis and the rest would have fought so hard for this land if they had known how many ugly motels and shopping centers would eventually stand on it. When I crossed the Brazos River all the motels were behind and the fog beneath the bridge was white as milk. Richmond, Wharton, El Campo, Edna, Victoria, all were still asleep, the only signs of life an occasional produce man unloading crates of cabbages in front of a grocery store.

The country was dim and lovely, as it always is at dawn or dusk, when the smells and colors have their full substance and have not been neutralized by the dust, the flatness, and the heat. Around 5 A.M. I turned on the radio and listened to a tired announcer out of Shreveport doggedly plug a hillbilly album called *The Teardrop Special*. The songs he played were almost as tired as he was, most of them third-rate renditions of old hillbilly staples by Hank Williams, Webb Pierce, and Kitty Wells. Hillbilly is a music of estrangement—the estrangement of country people who have moved to the city and not found the city good. Most of the songs are utterly banal, yet something of the emotional rawness of such people's lives comes through. Nostalgia is raised almost to the level of a passion—nostalgia for the homeplace, some happy rural seat where the familiar connections still hold, where there are no cheatin' hearts, honky-tonk angels, or one-sided loves.

After the music came the market reports; and by this time the lights had begun to come on in the kitchens of farmhouses along the road. In these parts, listening to the stock-market means finding out what yearlings are bringing in Ft. Worth, and how many shoats there are in Kansas City. In the houses just off the road the farmers and ranchers were buttoning their shirts and listening pessimistically, while

their wives put biscuits in the oven. Five-thirty in the morning is an awful time to be getting bad news, but those who
endure it to the end are rewarded with a snappy chicken
feed commercial and six or eight bars of "The Yellow Rose
of Texas," just to tie things off.

I breakfasted at Refugio, a small town on the grey coastal
pastures, fifteen miles or so inland from Copano Bay. The
glass of water that came with breakfast had more flavor
than the food—it was almost as bad as the water one gets in
Ft. Stockton, a desert community some nine hundred miles
to the west. To take my mind off the water I looked at the
morning paper and discovered that the President was enter-
taining various members of his cabinet at the LBJ. One or
two of the guests looked more tormented than entertained,
particularly Secretary Freeman, who was frantically
attempting to drive a cow someplace. A cattleman at the
oil-cloth table next to mine was considering that picture
with grim delight—a consolation, perhaps, for the price of
cattle.

South of Refugio I crossed the Aransas River. Six large
turkey buzzards were sitting in a tree by the bridge, waiting
patiently for something to get run over. I had an insane urge
to cable their whereabouts to Paramount, in case they were
finding themselves again at a loss for buzzards. The run to
Kingsville was otherwise uneventful, and the next seventy
miles even more so, for I was crossing the King Ranch.
There were no towns and no filling stations along that
stretch, though now and then one sighted one of the little
King Ranch communities to the west of the road. Usually
they consist of a gas pump, a score or so of green and white
houses, and a one-story stone schoolhouse.

The Gulf was not many miles away and the constant push
of the seawind had twisted the live-oak trees so that their
branches all pointed inland. In the Panhandle, I think of

Charles Goodnight, but in South Texas I think of Captain Richard King, who left his mark on the area so indelibly that even motorists on a national highway sometimes feel like trespassers for seventy miles. Happily, by eight o'clock I had got beyond the big ranch and into what is called the Magic Valley. A helicopter came buzzing over a row of skinny palm trees, and a Border Patrolman peered down at the road suspiciously, as if he expected the bar-ditches to be swarming with wetbacks.

The first of the Valley towns is called Raymondville. I stopped and had a piece of apricot pie in a place called the Texas Moon Cafe. There was a Clabber Girl baking powder sign nailed to the front wall—a relic of forties advertising seldom seen nowadays. The waitress was a plain-faced woman who had her hair put up in an old-fashioned hair-net. There was only one other customer, an old man in clean khakis who sat at the counter staring at a half-glass of Lone Star beer as a chess player might stare at a chess board. When I stood up to pay I asked the waitress if there was anything special in Raymondville that a person ought to see.

"I tell you, what I'd like to see is the city limit sign goin' out," she said. "You either got to be pore or ignert to stay in a place like this."

"The hell you say," the old man said, carefully pouring a little more beer from bottle to glass. "You ain't lived here long enough to know what you're talkin' about. I guess you'd rather go up to Houston and get killed on them freeways." He contemplated his glass with an offended air.

"I guess an old widder woman like me ain't gonna be too happy anywhere," the waitress replied, somewhat intimidated. "Anyhow I wouldn't trade Upshur County for this whole valley down here. You ever been through Gladewater?"

She was asking me, but the old man didn't notice.

"No, and I ain't in no hurry to go," he said.

I had been through Gladewater that spring and said I thought it was lovely country.

"Aw, yeah, it's right pretty in the spring," she said, staring at the counter a moment with a look full of memory. Then she caught herself and gave me my change.

"I hope that pie wasn't too old," she said. "We don't sell much aypercot."

"That pie was cooked sometime this fall," the old man said, tilting his bottle carefully so that the last drops of beer would drain into the glass. "I don't remember it being here last summer."

&

IN RAYMONDVILLE I BEGAN TO see the vivid roadside grocery stores that are characteristic of the Valley. The counters are heaped with cabbages, cucumbers, green peppers, yellow squash, beans and onions and melons, all of which create a great sense of abundance. At Harlingen I turned east and took a brief side trip to the hamlet of Rio Hondo, hoping to find the filling station where Nelson Algren once spent so much time shelling blackeyed peas. I had in mind asking the Texas Institute of Letters to make it a literary shrine. I located several likely candidates, but positive identification was difficult and I soon gave up and drove on down the lower Valley, through the city of Brownsville and across the Rio Grande into Matamoros. A border is always a temptation.

American suburbia had managed to push its way only about a mile into Mexico. The apartment buildings on the broad avenue near the river were homogeneous and modern, but as one approached the center of town the streets grew narrower and the smell of cooking grew stronger. Near the central square I encountered a small but extremely passionate brass band, made up mostly of teenagers. They were playing military music with demonic fervor. I parked and angled away on foot, but the band attached itself to me and pursued me closely all through downtown Matamoros. Now and then I would lose it for a few minutes, but despite the noise of seven trumpets it always managed to sneak up on me again. After a time I dodged into a little grocery store called the Miscilinea Ruiz, where I drank a Coke and read Mexican comic books while the band marched around outside.

When I emerged, a taxi was waiting for me. The driver, a pleasant and ingenious man, promised to find all sorts of dirtiness for me and proved his ingenuity at once by managing to drive three miles while transporting me to a grocery store two blocks from our starting point. To the rear of the store, amid huge, fragrant stalks of bananas, I met a nervous little grocer who took me back in a corner behind a pile of cabbages and produced a cigar-box full of very low class erotica. The most amusing item in the collection was a piece called *The Mishandled Housemaid*—the story was set in post-war Paris but the volume was delightfully and incongruously illustrated with photogravures of Grecian lads and ladies complexly entangled in the Parthenon. I paid the banana-man for his trouble, but declined purchase. My taxi driver, a little offended, asked me if I wanted to go out to Boy's Town. Six hundred girls, he said. All clean.

One does not go far in Matamoros without beginning to appreciate the dust-cutting effects of pavement. The whole of Boy's Town and the pastures of scraggly mesquite surrounding it were coated in a thick layer of white dust. My driver took me to a place called the Cabaret Two X, where, he assured me, the girls were beautiful and absolutely immaculate. It was noon and extremely hot. The bar was empty except for a somnolent bartender and some clean tile tables. I emphasized that I was only in the market for Carta Blanca, but the point was ignored.

For the first few minutes, however, the Cabaret Two X was one of the most beautifully quiet places I had ever seen. The bar was clean and cool and opened onto a patio where one could see the hot sun beating down on the dusty bushes. I was reminded of Faulkner's remark in the *Paris Review*, about how convenient a job in a whorehouse could be for a writer. I had found the ideal place to write a short story, and was a little chagrined not to have one in mind.

Unfortunately, despite my protests, the bartender insisted on waking up one of the girls. Her name was Carmilla and when she staggered in, my taxi driver rattled his glass in embarrassment. She was neither beautiful nor immaculate, and only love or the omnivorous horniness of adolescence could have transformed her into a palatable sexual object. I apologized for having been the innocent cause of her being awakened; she made a few derogatory remarks and went back to bed. The bar settled back into its lovely quiet and I had another Carta Blanca, hoping a short story would occur to me. But something, probably Texas, was pressing too hard on my consciousness and in a few more minutes I left and crossed back over the Rio Grande.

🐨

WHEN I CLEARED CUSTOMS, a simple process on that border, it was 1:30 P.M. and eighty-nine degrees Fahrenheit in the shade of the customs shed. All Texas lay before me—literally. I picked up Highway 281 right where it begins and drove west, through La Paloma, Los Indios, Santa Maria. Teams of braceros were at work in the green cabbage fields. I drove all the way up the Valley to Rio Grande City, a dusty little town that has been the scene of several celebrated border battles, some of them quite recent. Then I turned back to McAllen and drove north through the orchard country. The Valley's charm is only fully evident in the evening, when dusk touches the orchards and the white sky becomes a deep liquid blue. As the day waned I passed Captain King's ranch again and saw scattered bunches of Santa Gertrudis cattle, their red coats shining in the late sunlight.

I stopped for the night in Alice. All afternoon I had been in that part of the state where life is cheapest, particularly Mexican life. No part of the state has a bloodier history or, indeed, a bloodier potential. Should the laborers of the Valley ever acquire a militant leader, one smart enough to avoid arrest or assassination, the border country might again be as dangerous as it was a century ago.

In Alice, things were peaceful, if not quiet. The teenagers seemed to be using the car-horns to exchange messages in code. I dropped in at a hillbilly dance-hall, but it was virtually empty. In the Mexican part of town, crowds of kids were about, drinking orange soda pop in front of tiny corner grocery stores. When I was a very small boy my father took me with him on a cattle-buying trip to a ranch in the all-but-impenetrable brush country near Alice. I could not understand how the vaqueros could find cattle in such a tangle of mesquite. My fancy motel was a far cry from the old boomer's hotel we had stayed in on that trip, a hostelry where the bedbugs were many times more numerous than the guests.

At one point on that trip it had been necessary for my father to leave me in the car, out in the middle of a vast, brushy pasture, while he went off on horseback with the owner of the ranch. While I waited apprehensively for his return, four greasy and mirthful Mexican cowboys filtered out of the brush as if by magic and loped up to the car. They were as delighted to see me as I was appalled to see them:

they dismounted and crowded around the car, talking in rapid Spanish. At that time I knew little enough English, and only one poor phrase of Tex-Mex: "*No sabe.*" I told them *no sabe* several times while they tried to tempt me out of the car with offers of ropes, spurs, and food. Unfortunately, all they had in their saddlebags were a few mountain oysters (calves' testicles) that had been lightly scorched in a branding fire several days before. I was not tempted, and when the novelty of finding me wore off, the vaqueros mounted up and vanished silently into the brush.

❦

BY NINE THE NEXT MORNING I was in San Antonio, the one truly lovely city in the state. Already the doors of the many small bars were propped open to the soft air. I walked by the San Antonio River awhile and had breakfast at a cafe by the waterside, only a few blocks from the Alamo. The green water flowed quietly past and on toward the grey salty Gulf, where I had been but the morning before. When I finished eating I walked by the Alamo and over to the little square where sometimes the friendly old bums of O. Henry still gather on winter mornings to take the sun. We have never really captured San Antonio, we Texans—somehow the Spanish have managed to hold it. We have attacked with freeways and motels, shopping centers, and now that H-bomb of boosterism, HemisFair; but happily the victory still eludes us. San Antonio has kept an ambiance that all the rest of our cities lack.

❦

I THREADED MY WAY OUT, STILL on 281, and was soon in (hallelujah) the Hill Country, homeland of our President. On the radio the Reverend Carl McIntire and his colleague Amen Charlie were dishing out a familiar version of the gospel: half jeremiad, half appeal for funds. Old style preachin' on the blood is going out now, both on the radio and in the churches. Most small-towners prefer a mild Protestantism, a sort of theological Librium. It is mostly old-age pensioners who keep the Reverend McIntire on the air, and he in turn helps strengthen them in their conviction that America is teetering on the edge of the Pit.

In Johnson City I stopped and searched for cafes, hoping I might find a cowboy named Chuck Richey, who had moved there from my hometown. Not long ago, in a national magazine, Chuck had come forth with the interesting theory that intelligent men are likely to have big ears, the way some intelligent horses do. The bigger the ears (presumably), the smarter the man—a standard that would make President Johnson a universal genius. Unfortunately, Chuck was not to be found, and after a bit of aimless exploration in Johnson City, I turned toward Austin. Had I felt more diligent I might have made an attempt to see the LBJ ranch, but besides being of limited diligence I had been by the ranch a few months before and the parts that were visible from the road were no more verdant than any other scrub-country pasture. There are a great many pseudo-ranches in Texas and they don't vary enough to justify much investigation. Some just have more telephones than others.

🐚

PHYSICALLY, AUSTIN IS A PLEASANT town. Dusk found me in a drive-in on Guadalupe Street. I had been on my way out, but the marquee had promised an all-new height in fright and might and I decided to rest awhile and take in *Hercules and the Haunted World.* It starred Reg Park, surely one of the funniest and least cerebral of the neo-musclemen. As Hercules he proved somewhat too stolid, so while he descended into the nether world I got out and had a look at the refreshment lounge—itself a nether world of a sort.

Most of the teenagers in the drive-in had abandoned their cars and were packed into a special television room which the management had thoughtfully provided for those who couldn't stand movies. *The Dick Van Dyke Show* was on and the kids were annoyed because the screams of Hercules' imperiled heroine kept drowning it out. On the TV a girl in an off-the-shoulder black dress was singing:

> *Way down yonder in Louise-ee-anna*
> *Just about a mile from Texarkana,*
> *In them old cottonfields back home . . .*

Her cleavage was impressive, though probably if she had attempted to pick cotton in that gown it would have been even more so. The lounge had a large plate glass window, through which one could see some fifty feet of heroine. She, also, was décolleté, and was about to be sacrificed to a vampire. The kids were not interested in either girl, but in their own reflections, which flickered onto the plate glass whenever the screen outside momentarily darkened. So many levels of sexual posturing were visible at once that it veritably swamped the senses. For a moment I felt myself the ultimate spectator, an audience within an audience within an audience. Then it occured to me how eerie it would be if someone were watching me, and I got my car and left.

❦

IT WAS A CLEAR, WARM NIGHT, with still a tinge of afterglow beyond the Austin hills. At Lampasas I picked up 281 again and followed it north, through Evant, Hamilton, Hico,

Stephenville. The moon was high and white over the Brazos Valley—it made me think of the Texas Moon Cafe, and of the widow woman and her argumentative customer, their good times mostly gone. Soon I crossed the Brazos, its channels silvered by the moon. As always, crossing it there, I looked down, hoping to see John Graves pass underneath me in his canoe—for the Brazos is his river and one expects him there.

In Mineral Wells I parked beside the towering, empty Baker Hotel and slept awhile in the car. I awoke an hour before dawn and had the highway to Jacksboro all to myself. There a lone filling-station man was hosing down his pavement. The radio stations in Ft. Worth had not yet come awake. Some twenty miles beyond Jacksboro I entered my home country. In the darkness to the west, a mile and a half off the road, lay the old McMurtry homestead, the land my grandparents had settled on in the 1880s. I topped a ridge and in the clear 5:30 darkness could see the lights of my hometown, fifteen miles away. Through my college years, topping that ridge had always given me a great sense of being home, but time had diminished the emotion and I had begun to suspect that home was less a place than an empty page. Still, it was good to see that the lights were still in their place on the horizon. In some ways the town seems more remote and isolated now than when I lived there, and in time I imagine the remoteness and isolation of the small towns of the West will constitute their most positive appeal.

I breakfasted with my parents and was on my way again by eight o'clock. The breeze was coming down from the Rockies, rather than up from the Gulf, and was consequently much cooler. In order to avoid Wichita Falls, I took a short-cut to the northwest. Lubbock, Amarillo, and Wichita Falls are the three principal cities of the Texas plain—cities that I find uniformly graceless and unattractive. In summer they are dry and hot, in winter cold, dusty, and windswept; the population is rigidly conformist on the surface and seethes underneath with imperfectly suppressed malice.

As I was driving through an oil-town called Electra I passed a senior citizens' home and saw an old man in a red mackinaw sitting in a wheelchair on the south side of the building, in the lee of the wind. His name was Jesse Brewer, and since he had been my first friend in the world, I swerved off the road and stopped. During the war, when most of the younger men were gone, Jesse had cowboyed for my father for a while. I have always suspected that his real job was to keep me out of danger, or at least out of the way.

When I walked up and said hello he was chewing tobacco and looking out across the brown rolling country to the southwest. "How you doin', Larry?" he said, no wit surprised to see me. Then, looking cautiously around to see who might be watching, he spat tobacco juice on the roots of a domesticated prickly pear that was growing by the wall. The look around was a habit formed in ranch houses, where women were apt to take unkindly to men who chewed.

Jesse was in his nineties, and had sunk a little farther into his Mackinaw in the five years since I had last seen him. His spirits, however, were excellent. He at once proceeded to ask me all the questions that are standard in the cattle country. How were my father's cattle? Was there any grass? Where was I living?

When I told him Houston he made a grimace of commiseration. "Hard to breathe down there, ain't it?" he said, convinced, as most plainsmen are, that any place south of Waco must be a malarial swamp.

As we were chatting, a nurse came out, decreed he had had enough sun, and briskly wheeled him in for a morning of television. For a man who had followed the cow, it seemed a dull end. We waved and I drove on, and did not see Jesse alive again.

꩜

AT ESTELLINE I CROSSED THE Red River, and knew I was on the plains. In Clarendon, a town teeming with McMurtrys, I stopped for a succession of lunches with my uncles and aunts. Had I cared to draw on cousins I could have prolonged the feeding for several days, but I was coming into the homestretch and wanted to drive. High above, the thunderheads were blowing south. I passed through Claude, and to my surprise the water-tower still said THALIA. Between Amarillo and Dumas I saw a small herd of antelope grazing on the brown plains, obviously the pets of some rancher with a little grass to spare. At Dumas I turned due west toward Dalhart. There were some forty-five minutes of sun left, and almost eighty miles between me and the New Mexico line. I was tired and had begun to feel a little flat. The drive was almost over, and I had not seen anything that would lead me to any startling new assessment of Texas. The long, sloping fall sunlight fell beautifully on the green winter wheatfields east of Dalhart; in the gullies and breaks of the rougher country I saw seedling mesquite spreading up out of the draws in irregular lines. The persistent mesquite. When my father was a boy there were none in Archer County, almost four hundred miles to the south—by the time my son is old there will probably be mesquite on the slopes of Pikes Peak.

Perhaps that was going to be the only discovery of the trip: mesquite in Hartley County. The drive merely pointed up two things that I had already known: the brush thrives, and the small towns wither, their sap draining into the cities year after year. In my own hometown, population 2,000, there was an old man named Taylor who lived in a mansion just across a sudan field from our house. His fortune was made, and he spent his time reading. When I went to bed at night I could see the light in his library window, and when I awoke in the morning it would often still be burning. At four in the afternoon he drove down the hill in his Packard and got his mail. In the junkpiles behind his house were piles of book catalogues, mostly English. He was, I suppose, the village intellectual, a figure of yesteryear—defunct now like Buffalo Bill. His successors have all gone to the city: the brainy, the imaginative, the beautiful, even the energetic. None of them can find much reason for staying in the towns.

⚜

WHEN I PASSED THROUGH DALHART the sun was not more than ten minutes above the wheatfields. I had forty miles to go, into a clear Panhandle sunset. When I drove through Texline and out to the marker at the border, the sun had been down twenty minutes and afterglow circled the entire horizon with pink and rose. The sky, which had seemed clear, really held a thin, almost invisible glaze of cloud, and streamers of afterglow reddened the clouds as far east as one could see. I got out and stood by the marker a minute in the biting north wind, 1,073 miles from the Rio Grande bridge in Brownsville. It was only thirty-five degrees, a warm fall evening for the plains.

Clayton, New Mexico was only six miles up the road. For the sake of symmetry I should have gone across and spent an hour, but I was not tempted: there is no place in Clayton as pleasant as the Cabaret Two X. What was hard was not going on to Denver. You can't see the Rockies from Texline, but you can sense them, and the wind brought me visions of Colorado: of couples in Denver walking in the cold clean evening air in the park below the gold-domed Capitol.

But my destination lay in the other direction, and I turned my back on Denver and drove slowly into Texline, rather dreading the forty-mile return trip to Dalhart. As soon as I got rolling the dread fell away: the plains were lovely as they darkened, and I cannot but love the plains, nor cross them without the sense that I am crossing my own past. I curved back down to Dalhart through the wind the trailherders bucked, and the last few miles, with the lights twinkling ahead of me on the plain, were among the best of the trip. It remained only to perform some *acte symbolistique* to give the drive coherence, tie the present to the past. I stopped at a cafe in Dalhart and ordered a chicken fried steak. Only a rank degenerate would drive 1,500 miles across Texas without eating a chicken fried steak. The cafe was full of boys in football jackets, and the jukebox was playing an odious number called "Billy Broke My Heart in Walgreen's and I Cried All the Way to Sears."

The waitress was a thin, sad-eyed woman with hands that looked like she had used them to twist barbed wire all her life. She set the steak in front of me and went wearily back to the counter to get a bottle of ketchup. The meat looked like a piece of old wood that had had perhaps one coat of white paint in the thirties and then had had that sanded off by thirty years of Panhandle sandstorms.

"Here," the waitress said, setting the ketchup bottle down. "I hope that steak's done enough. There ain't nothin' like steak when you're hungry, is there, son?"

"No, ma'am, there ain't," I said.

THAT NIGHT I DROVE ON to Dodge City. In two days I had come from the Nueces to the Arkansas, a distance the trail-drivers would have been pressed to cover in as many months. I would have liked, while I was at it, to drive the state east to west—from Texarkana to El Paso—but I had neither the time nor the money, and anyway the prospect of driving back from El Paso was too depressing.

Seeing the state whole requires one, of course, to take some account of those dark portions of it which lie east of Dallas. I have had, admittedly, few opportunities to observe East Texans in their native habitat, and, since those of them who stray from beneath the pines soon learn to disguise their origins, I have had to glean what I can about the people there from the works of William Humphrey and William Goyen. I did, however, have one singularly good opportunity for direct observation when, in 1962, I attended the twenty-seventh Old Fiddlers' Reunion, an event held annually in Athens, Texas. In order that the region known as East Texas not be entirely slighted in these pages, I should like, in the following section, to record the impressions I gathered that day.

The Old Soldier's Joy

ATHENS IS A MEDIUM-sized East Texas county-seat town, located some seventy miles southeast of Dallas. It lies between the Neches and the Trinity, in country that is not too heavily wooded. In May, when the Old Fiddlers' Reunion is held, the country is green and clean-smelling, with a little pine in the smell.

I arrived around nine in the morning, early enough that the air was still cool. At the red light by the southeast corner of the courthouse square I stuck my head out of the car window, expecting to hear the screech of country fiddles. Instead, I heard a vastly amplified citybilly voice singing "Don't Let the Stars Get in Your Eyes" (don't let the moon break your haw-art . . .), a sound so loud and so quintessentially downhome that I was momentarily paralyzed with emotion, or something, and had to be honked into a parking place.

On the east side of the courthouse there was a big pine-lumber platform, upon which the fiddling and string-band contests would be held. The platform was occupied just then by a Mr. Red Rogers and his band, a group that seemed committed exclusively to the music of Bob Wills. I had not driven all the way from Ft. Worth to hear such a decadent strain of hillbilly, so I hurried off to look for old fiddlers.

When the substantial barrier of the courthouse was between me and Mr. Rogers' music I felt better about things and stopped to survey the scene. A small, quietly lyrical group was gathered nearby, and on the extreme periphery of it stood the first old fiddler I was to talk with: Mr. Clarence McGraw of West Los Angeles, California. The group proper consisted of two fiddlers (one of them Mr. McGraw's brother), one guitar player, one policeman, and two totally committed listeners. The fiddlers and the guitar player were playing "Cripple Creek," and the listeners gave the music their gravest attention. Mr. Clarence was fiddling too, but not "Cripple Creek." He was off to one side, fiddling angrily to himself. He looked exceptionally clean and vigorous for a man his age, or any age. His grey khakis were brand clean and strongly starched. He kept one eye on his brother, who had a curious way of tucking his fiddle under his solar plexus, rather than under his chin. I had a notebook in my hand, and when he noticed it he immediately began to fiddle in my direction.

"You're a reporter for the paper, ain't you?" he asked, and then quickly turned aside and scratched out a few disgusted measures to himself.

Before I had time to deny it, he was on the attack.

"What I'd like to know is how a feller goes about getting' an *account* of this here fiddlin'," he said. "This here's about got me whupped."

"How so?" I asked.

"I come here last year and fiddled," he said. "By god when I got home I wrote three separate letters back, askin' them to send me an account of how she all come out. I never got nothin'. Not a damn fare-thee-well. You ask me, this here's the ass of nowhere."

About that time the group finished "Cripple Creek" and quietly began to break up. The policeman made mild protests.

"Hey," he said. "Y'all play that 'Under the Double Eagle.' Y'all ain't played that yet."

But the group demurred and went their way. The McGraw brothers got into an inconclusive argument over who would use which fiddle-bow in the contests to come. Mr. Clarence was bitterly self-deprecatory and said it made no difference, he could fiddle about as well without a bow. His brother, a quiet man, seemed inclined to let him try.

When the McGraws left I decided to look for the man in charge of the contests, so as to know what was happening when. A farmer was sitting a few feet away on the courthouse steps, resting himself beneath the long morning shadow of the courthouse and the smaller but more portable shadow of an old felt hat that in its day had soaked up a lot of head sweat and dust and Rose hair oil. When I asked him about the contests he was thrown slightly off balance.

"Why, they're liable to start any time," he said sadly. "Pretty soon, I 'spect. Ole Bob Hall's the man to ask about that, he'll have the papers on it. Just go up and ask him, first time you catch a chanct. Bob won't care."

I thanked him and said I would, but I didn't. Though I found the man he was talking about, I never could quite catch the chanct.

❦

BY TEN O'CLOCK THERE WERE swarms of fiddlers about, and not all of them old. Indeed, the most popular fiddler present that day was a local youngster named Texas Shorty, a fiddle-playing arriviste if there ever was one. He was in his mid-twenties, short and stocky, and dressed in the artificial-pearl-button and near-gabardine of a minor hillbilly entertainer— the sort who, ages ago, would have drawn only the faintest crackle of applause from Horace Heidt's applause meter.

I listened to him awhile and his fiddling seemed as passionless and repetitive as the tinkle from a moderately well-made music box. While he fiddled, a female relative circulated through the crowd, selling glossy pictures of him and letting it be known that he would autograph them. I would have thought a career of Saturday-night shitkicking at the Big D Jamboree would have been the summit of Shorty's ambition, but apparently I am no judge of fiddling. I found out later that he had just returned from a tour of England— a tour sponsored by the State Department. The news cooled me a bit on the New Frontier, but before the day was over I was forced to admit that Shorty did have *something*. What he had was tenacity: all day long he fiddled steadily, now here, now there, but always fiddling. "Sally Goodin'" was all he knew on earth and all he needed to know. When I left at nine that night he was up on the big platform, sawing sturdily away.

❦

AFTER THE McGRAW GROUP BROKE up I wandered back around the platform side of the courthouse, looking at faces in the crowd. There was a curious group of teenage pseudo-thugs: they wore identical cheap straw hats and had them pulled so far down over their eyes that they had to walk leaning backwards in order to see. And there was the youngest and least confident sailor I've ever seen. He had on a white uniform and stood around all day wishing he could go home and take it off before someone challenged him to a fight. The country people were there too. Old-timers sat on the courthouse steps, chewing tobacco. Now and then one would rise and hobble painfully over to some bush, spit his tobacco juice into it, and hobble back. Infants lay on spread-out quilts under the trees, sucking their blue-plastic bottles while their grandmothers or little sisters sat by and shooed the flies.

Around eleven o'clock Mr. Rogers and his fellows ceased trying to scale the heights of Bob Wills and the old fiddlers' contest started. Happily, it was soon over. Only about twenty old men were entered, and each fiddled only two short numbers. By noon they had all put their fiddles away and retired to shade trees or the homes of relatives. I was glad. The contest was like *Paradise Lost:* no one could have wished it longer.

As they stepped up, one by one, to fiddle, the old men reminded me of the superannuated ministers one sees in the congregations of southern churches. On special Sundays like Christmas and Easter the old Brother may be asked as a matter of courtesy to stand up and say a prayer or lead a benediction. Now and then one will get up and do the job briskly and sit down, but more often the old preacher will rise shakily, tremble, work his jaws a little, quaver out a beginning, perhaps forget what comes next, cry a little, desperately improvise a line or two, and, to the infinite relief of all, ashamedly slump down, more than ever aware that he has become too old to cut the mustard.

So it was with the old fiddlers. One or two sawed their way vigorously through "Turkey in the Straw" or "The Arkansas Traveller," but most didn't. Most quavered. A local man named Bunyard won the contest, and Mr. Clarence's brother came in third. Mr. Clarence's fiddling I missed. I went across the street to get a Coke and stopped to listen to a vulgar woman of high community standing who was sitting in front of the platform in a pre-parked Cadillac. She was talking loudly about the Burton-Taylor romance—the gist of her remarks was that Elizabeth Taylor ought to be spayed, else the menfolk of the entire Western world would soon be reduced to a state of slavering idiocy. When I got back to the platform Mr. Clarence was just coming down, and I asked him how he had done.

"Pitiful," he said. "My arm was too stiff on that first piece. I got to talkin' and never took enough warm-ups."

On the platform Uncle John Murdock of Rusk, Texas, was fiddling gallantly away at "The Old Soldier's Joy." He had not taken enough warm-ups either, or perhaps had taken too many. He was eighty-four years old and had roses painted on his fiddle.

Around lunchtime the old fiddlers were replaced by the LIGHTCRUST DOUGHBOYS, a hillbilly band of some renown. I remembered hearing them on the radio in the late forties. The personnel had probably changed, but as I remembered it they sang good energetic hillbilly, and I was prepared to like them. Their pink vests were something of a deterrent, however, and their humour (i.e., "Don't-go-around-with-another-man's-wife-unless-you-can-go-two-rounds-with-her-husband") was another. Their music moved steadily pop-ward until it was nudging Glenn Miller, at which point I found that my nostalgia had been overridden.

While the DOUGHBOYS were whirling through "Cimarron, Roll On" I wandered off in search of authentic East Texans and found one right away in the curious, friendly person of Colonel Colin Douglas. Colonel Douglas' black beard was easily the equal of Allen Ginsberg's, and went well with his short-topped California motorcycle boots. He was a local ranch owner and a traveled and experienced man. He had been in pictures in the twenties, he said, but had left them for the oil business at about the time Clark Gable did the opposite. In a few minutes the DOUGHBOYS finished and abruptly yielded the platform to a politician, a (now-forgotten) gubernatorial candidate who had slipped in to take advantage of the free people. He had more force than the old fiddlers, but considerably less poignance. The world, he said, was divided into two warring ideologies: the freedom lovers and the atheists. That elemental distinction established, he went on to draw a subtle parallel between himself and Abraham Lincoln (his subtlety consisted in not mentioning the latter by name). He had been born in a one-room cabin on the wrong side of the tracks, and as a boy had gone to school with cardboard in his shoes. He elaborated on that point for a while, shook a few hard-knuckled hands, eased himself into a white Cadillac, and vanished forever.

A local group got the platform and managed to hold it awhile, all of them singing as loudly as it is possible to sing through one's nose. Shortly, however, they were routed by the master of ceremonies, who announced that the young fiddlers' contest was about to begin. That meant that Texas Shorty was going to fiddle over the loudspeaker, a prospect that for me held small appeal. It was a hot afternoon and I was half in the mood to go home, but when I stopped to gas up a filling station man warned me against leaving too soon. He assured me that the real Fiddler's Day action had not yet begun. By nightfall, he said, there would be several thousand people around the square. There would be street-dancing, whiskey drinking and wild, wild women.

I was impressed and said I'd hang around. To pass the time I set out in search of Miss Zilla B. Elledge and her sister, two women of artistic bent who lived in the woods near Athens. For years, legend had it, they had lived in an old ex-mansion in the pines, keeping what house they kept in one room and slowly stripping the others down and burning them for firewood. A year or so earlier they had reportedly burned the last of the mansion, after which they moved into the chickenhouse. All I really knew about them was that Zilla B. had sent my friend John Graves a Christmas card with a red pepper tied to it and a note saying: "This is good, eat it." That was enough to make a search seem worthwhile, but unhappily the search proved futile. Some whittlers at a little country grocery store informed me that the girls were off in Mexico and were not due back until frost.

Disappointed, I drove to the nearby town of Corsicana and whiled away the afternoon in a second-run movie house. It was getting on toward the cool of the evening when I got back to Athens—the lawn and the streets were filling up with people, and the string band contest, my last and brightest hope, was just about to begin.

I went up on the platform to study the contest list, and the lineup of bands looked impressive. The FIDDLE SWING-STERS were to kick things off, followed more or less in order by such groups as the TEXAS RAMBLERS, the SHAWNEE WRAN-GLERS, the TEXAS BLUE EAGLES, and the TWILIGHT SERE-NADERS. I crept across the stage and squeezed into a corner on the south side. A big red snare drum sat on one side of me, and the three contest judges sat on the other.

The judges were stalwart men indeed: all day they hardly left their chairs. One was fat and looked complacent and the other two were thinner and looked vacant. Their judging methods seemed highly instinctive: none of them seemed to make the slightest effort to score performances, or even to keep track of who was performing, yet winners were announced almost immediately. While I was sitting near them a lady pressed herself against the chickenwire screen and asked Red Hayes, the nearest judge, if Texas Shorty was going to perform again.

"He's awful good, ain't he," the lady said.

"Yes, ma'am," Red said. "He sure plays that fiddle."

"Next time he comes on ask him to play the 'Tennessee

Waltz' for me, will you? My sister's crippled with arthritis, she's been that way ten years. We got her out here in the car and that's her favorite song."

"Lady, we can't take no requests," Red said. "I sure am sorry."

"Oh, you don't have to take none," she assured him. "Just tell Shorty Mrs. Muldrow wanted him to play that for her sister. Shorty won't mind. I've known Shorty's mother since she was a girl. We sure are proud of him around here."

About that time the TEXAS SWINGSTERS came on stage and began to plug in their numerous electric instruments. From the cut of their pink, sequined vests I supposed them to be DOUGHBOY imitators and got set to endure "Tuxedo Junction" on the Hawaiian guitar. Instead they played three polkas, and the contest was off to a wailing start.

Before the first polka died away I ceased paying the musicians any mind. I sat and looked off the platform at the people. The filling station man had been right: the people were coming. The courthouse lawn was solid full, and the street in front of the courthouse was filled to the center esplanade and was packing tighter. Those farthest from the platform were still in the sunlight, but most of the crowd stood within the cool widening shadow of the courthouse.

Looking down on all those shifting faces it was hard not to lapse into generalization. I was looking down, not just on East Texas, but on the South. The people below me were Southern: they had more in common regionally with the people who might gather on the courthouse lawns of Georgia and Alabama than with the Texans who lived in Lubbock, San Antonio, or El Paso. East Texans are moulded by the South, West Texans by the West, and the two cultures are no longer correspondent.

Below me was a fair sampling of the region's peasantry. It had not been dramatically destroyed, not smitten with a sword; but it was surely witnessing its own slow and ruinous depletion. In those people, the sap was drying, the seed withering. As they moved about beneath the insulating, isolating twang of the Swingster's steel guitar the sense one got was of lethargy and defeat, of apathy, not tragedy. The compelling if sometimes wicked grandeur of Sutpen and Sartoris was past, a grandeur of myth, of fictive or historical dream: there is little of it left in the present-day South. One would have had a hard time finding in that crowd the kind of faces that Walker Evans and Dorothea Lange photographed three decades ago, when our peasantry was enduring a harsher and more tragic trial. The faces below looked softer and less sharp, and the hard, austere grace had mostly eroded away.

❦

AS I WAS BRINGING THESE GLOOMY speculations into focus, something good finally happened on the platform. A young man named Johnny Grimble came on stage with his quartet. They were four good-natured local boys in khakis, and they didn't have a voltage-powered instrument of any kind. Apparently they had already tuned up, because they lit right into a song called "Rubber Dolly." If they had had nothing but their energy they would still have been better than any group I had heard that day. But besides energy, they had the sense to sing songs that meant something to them, and they were not too citified to swing their elbows and pat their feet. When "Rubber Dolly" was over the leader stepped to the microphone and sang a ballad with sex in it. One line was repeated over and over:

She called me Baaby, baa-by all night loong.

He had no great skill nor great concern with skill, but he had passion enough to transform a corny song and make it seem true. When he switched to

Have I told you lately that I love you . . .

the crowd responded to what was genuine and got quiet. The sun had dropped behind the courthouse. For the first time that day I felt I was hearing music that expressed the people around the platform, though more probably it was Johnny Grimble who expressed them. When he stepped back from the microphone the group swang into "Under the Double Eagle." I hoped that morning policeman was still around.

When the Grimble boys stepped down things deteriorated rapidly back to the level of the SWINGSTERS. The next two bands had so many steel guitars that my ears began to ring, and I left the platform. It seemed a good time to see what breed of men and women had come in for the street dancing.

Certainly East Texas womanhood was showing me its painful worst. All day I had not noticed a pretty woman around the bandstand, nor could I spot one in the evening crowd. A few were of the long-legged, gawky variety, but the majority were short straggle-haired farm women with dumpy breasts, thin legs, and fat behinds. There were a lot of town women around, but except for stiff permanent waves and more make-up they looked like the country women.

While I was walking through the crowd they turned on the yellow bulbs that had been strung above the street to light the dancing. Their strong, almost urinous glare contrasted with the soft dusk and gave colors of grotesquerie to the whole assemblage. A bunch of flabby-armed, hugely pregnant women stood by the curb, talking about their pregnancies. There was a concession stand, and a little booth next to it where they sold cotton candy and pennants and monkeys on strings, foam rubber dice to dangle from rear-view mirrors, raccoon tails and Confederate flags. Passing the booth, I saw a little barefooted, sandy-haired East Texas boy in overalls, standing with his obviously stonebroke, whiskey-breathed father. The little boy was staring with his whole being at one of the cheap telescopes on sale for $1.98. The purity of his want was too much to look upon. When the man beckoned, the boy followed, but one felt that for years part of him would remain right there, wanting that telescope. Part of me has remained there too, for the moment hangs in my mind—a glimpse of the beginnings of destruction, his or mine or everyone's, in that real and terrible hunger for a trivial thing.

The older boys in the crowd cheered me somewhat. They were hungry for sex and were clustered around the teenage girls. Then I went into the courthouse to get a drink of water and ran into a family of idiots. I had been seeing one of them all day, a taciturn boy-man with a concave face and receded nose. One could have laid a rule from forehead to chin without touching either his lips or his nose. Suddenly, grouped on the steps like freaks from the old Tod Browning movie, were four more like him, one of them an old lady and one a pregnant girl who looked no older than fourteen. The crowd just wasn't working out for me.

On the platform a group called the WESTERN ALLSTARS was having its try. They sported a female vocalist, a small, thin-legged girl in a grimy looking black skirt and a tasseled blouse.

I'm driftin' in-to deep wa-ter . . .

she sang, a faint Kitty Wells timbre in her voice. The folk listened in silence—or were they the folk? Once the concept of folk carried with it an implicit relation to the soil: the folk lived on and worked the land. Now they are drifting, surely, but not toward deeper waters—toward the same suburbs and television swamps in which the cowboys were bogged.

That day I had driven from Ft. Worth to Dallas, through Dallas, and on to Athens. Of the hundred miles I traveled, fifty had been suburbia. I had driven along the new Stemmons Freeway and got the commuter's view of the Big D skyline, with the bright tincan facades of the skyscrapers flashing in the morning sun. They tapered upward, at that time, to the ultimate Southwestern phallus, the shaft with the light in its head above the Republic National Bank. The Flying Red Horse that had once reared unchallenged above all Texas was far below. I drove up Commerce Street, so aptly named, past Neiman-Marcus, its *ne plus* produce and *ultra* customers beautifully juxtaposed to the beer joints, wine-bars and shoeshine parlors of South Ervay. I drove out Second Avenue, past the Fair Grounds, a Goodwill store, a D.A.V. store, twenty second-hand furniture stores, numerous used car lots, a Negro picture show, two junk-auto yards, forty hamburger stands and the Kaufman Pike Drive-In. Behind me was where the folk had drifted, to Neiman's and Second Avenue, South Ervay and the Stemmons Freeway and the thirty miles of cottonpatch suburbia between Ft. Worth and Dallas. It was little wonder that the farms around Athens had a wilting look, even though the grass was green and the air the air of spring.

🍃

THE LAST BAND I HEARD THAT night was the TWILIGHT SERE-NADERS, a group unique in two respects. First, in regard to instrumentation: they were far and away the most elaborately equipped group to appear, with over a dozen pieces and everything electric but the fiddle.

Second, and more remarkable, they had for a vocalist the one really lovely woman I saw that day.

She came on stage with her daughter, who was to accompany her. They sat just beyond the judges, at my end of the stage. She was to sing only one song, and sat very quietly, her hands folded in her lap, during the long half-hour it took the SERENADERS to get their twelve instruments plugged in and tuned. I watched her from amid the empty instrument cases. She was in her early forties, still shapely and high-breasted, a calm, graceful, brown-haired woman. All day I had watched graceless bodies and resigned faces, but her face was not resigned, merely sorrowful. Her name was Obera Waters. Though she sat with a quiet, pleasant look on her face, what one noticed most in her was a combination of melancholy and weariness—the tired, composed weariness of someone who has lived a long while in the love of people whose capacities were smaller than her own.

When Mrs. Waters stood up to sing, I noticed that she was missing two lower front teeth. She sang "Standing In the Shadows," and sat back down. One of the musicians came over and squatted by me for a minute. He put up his electric banjo and took out an electric mandolin. Underneath the instrument was a little sheaf of song lyrics, typed on variety-store tablet paper and held together with a paper-clip. The song on top was "I Am Weak But Thou Art Strong," a song that simply begs for mandolin accompaniment.

He plugged in the mandolin and the SERENADERS began their elaborate tune-up—only this time it was too elaborate. The strain of all those instruments was finally too much for the circuits, and several fuses blew. The SERENADERS were reduced to a few discordant tinkles. It took them twenty minutes to get the fuses replaced, and in the interim I learned that Texas Shorty was up next, with Red Rogers in the wings. The street dance seemed suddenly not worth waiting for, and I left. When I walked off the platform Mrs. Waters still sat calmly in the chair, her hands folded again and her face still lovely and tired.

※

IN LESS THAN AN HOUR I was back on Second Avenue. I crossed Dallas and stopped for a cheeseburger at a little beer joint near the Circle. Sitting next to me at the counter was a good-natured guy in a green Dr Pepper Bottling Co. uniform—he was a baseball fan, and lacked several more teeth than Mrs. Waters. A girl called to him from a booth and he grabbed his two bottles of Pearl and left.

If Dallas is good for nothing else, it is a useful divider. I had been in the South all day, but as I turned toward Ft. Worth I re-entered the West—for me, always a good feeling. Ahead, north to Canada and west to the Coast lay what to me is the most exciting stretch of land in America. Despite its rudeness, newness, rawness, it is not worn out, not yet filled, not yet exhausted.

If one loves the West it is sometimes deeply moving to drive along one of its rims and sense the great spread of country that lies before one: West Texas, New Mexico and Colorado, Wyoming, the Dakotas, Utah, Arizona, Montana and Idaho, Nevada, Oregon and Washington, and the long trough of California; with the names of rivers and cities and highways now binding the land like the old trails which once led to Oregon or Santa Fe—now it is Highway 40 and Highway 80 and Highway 66 that lead one from the Mississippi to the Pacific, to Cheyenne or to Denver, to Phoenix, El Paso, Los Angeles, or San Francisco.

On the rims of the West—and perhaps, in America, only there—one can still know for a moment the frontier emotion, the loneliness and the excitement and the sense of an openness so vast that it still challenges—in Gatsbian phrase—our capacity for wonder.

I can summon no wonder for what lies between Dallas and Washington. The South is memories, memories—it cannot help believing that yesterday was better than tomorrow can possibly be. Some of the memories are extraordinarily well packaged, it is true, but when a place has been reduced in its own estimation no amount of artful packaging can hide the gloom. I hope Mr. Clarence stays out there in West Los Angeles; his description of Athens, Texas, struck me as very apt. And when I think of Obera Waters, who is left there still, it is as a rare and weary reminder of a people's departing grace.

Love, Death, & the Astrodome

A VERSION OF the previous chapter was published some years ago in *The Texas Quarterly*, a publication edited in Austin by the ghost of William Lyon Phelps. A number of correspondents suggested that I was no fit appreciator of East Texas pastoralism, and probably they were right. A version of *this* chapter was published some years ago in *The Texas Observer*, a publication also edited in Austin, I assume by wraiths and elves. A number of correspondents suggested that I had been frivolous and presumptuous to speak so disparagingly of the Dome, and probably they too are right. As it happens, frivolity and presumptuousness are qualities the Texas literary scene has always lacked. I merely thought to remedy that lack, and the Dome provided a compelling occasion.

The first promising rumour I heard about the Harris County Domed Stadium was that it was going to be large enough that the Shamrock Hotel could be put inside it. Great, I thought—assuming, naturally, that the powers that be would take advantage of such an opportunity. At last a real solution to the Shamrock problem seemed to lie at hand. Forty-five million dollars is a respectable sum, but who would cavil if it got that hotel out of sight?

A year or so later, with sinking heart, I realized that the Dome-builders had somehow missed the mark. The Shamrock continued to blot out a considerable portion of Houston's southern horizon, while a short distance away the huge white dome poked soothingly above the summer heat haze like the working end of a gigantic roll-on deodorant. Form, I supposed, was following function. We needed a Dome so Houston's sports fans wouldn't get so damp and sweaty.

It seemed neither wise nor fair. The weather in Houston is certainly oppressive, but then sports fans probably deserve and perhaps even require the bad weather they get. Braving frostbite and sunstroke helps keep their sadistic and masochistic tendencies in balance. Increasing their comfort might only make them meaner.

Besides, pallid though the argument may appear, it seemed a bit conscienceless for a city with leprous slums, an inadequate charity hospital, wretched public transportation and numerous other cultural and humanitarian deficiencies to sink more than thirty-one million dollars in public funds into a ball-park. (It was not, however, surprising: Houston is the kind of boom town that will endorse any amount of municipal vulgarity so long as it has a chance of making money. Building, hereabouts, has traditionally been a form of stealing, and however questionable the motive, it does insure that all sort of public marvels get built.)

❦

AT ANY RATE, THOUGH THE world may by now have forgotten the occasion, the Astrodome did open in the spring of 1965. The President attended the opening game, as did a constellation of lesser celebrities, and one could make a wicked little anthology of the things famous people had to say about the place. For a time, in Houston, the Astrodome was not just news, it was the only news. Texas was generally agog, and Dallas was feverish with civic envy. The letters columns of *The Dallas Morning News* were soon clogged with plaintive little epistles telling the editors how much better life would be if only Dallas had a dome. For a time there was even a move afoot to dome the Cotton Bowl.

I was somewhat slow in getting to the Dome, myself. Summer rolled around and the fact that I still hadn't been was leaving me more and more disadvantaged in conversations. It was like not having read McLuhan. "You simply have to see it to believe it," I was frequently told.

Finally I went, and five minutes after I walked inside I knew I could have believed it perfectly well without ever going near it. From the parking lot on, it was *echt*-Texas. By the time I came to this realization, however, I was four levels above the field, on a fast escalator, surrounded by a convention of National Press Photographers, their Rolleis, and their wives. Our tour guide, a pleasant, intelligent young lady, shepherded us out into what is called the Upper Stands and allowed us to sit down a few minutes and adjust to the altitude. By sitting us down until we had sort of come to terms with the size of the Dome most of us escaped the brief, sometimes unpleasant sense of disorientation that often afflicts visitors when they first enter.

Even sitting down I felt a little bit uncomfortable, and my trouble was not vertigo (though vertigo did cause one lady in the party to hurry back to the ramps). Far below us the Astros were taking batting practice, and while I could see the balls being hit I was too high up to hear the crack of the bat. The cause of my first discomfort, I think, was that the vast amount of physical space in the Dome is somehow out of proportion with the amount of psychological space. In that sense it is indeed *echt*-Texas. Some levels of the stadium are about as psychologically roomy as a sardine can. Fortunately the Dome itself is a clean, impressive piece of engineering, and does much to alleviate the sense of suffocation that can come on one in the clubs and restaurants.

❦

AT THIS TIME THE DOME still had its original grass, though much of it had already died and been painted a strange ungrassy green. There was a stretch in deep center field that looked as arid as the range along the Pecos, and a week before my visit the circus had trampled the infield into a green-tinted dirt. I am told it was an odd feeling to watch a circus in which the aerialists were a hundred feet below one.

When I had seen the Skyblazer Restaurant, the Countdown Cafeteria, and the Astrodome Club I quit the tour and drifted down five or six levels to the Domeskellar, where I refreshed myself with a poor-boy sandwich. The Domeskellar was like something in a baseball stadium—a place where one could buy a hot dog and a beer and sit and watch the game. The management so clearly regarded it as a plebian eatery that they hadn't bothered to fix it up much, whereas the other places are so fixed up they leave one gasping for breath.

The one great advantage to the Domeskellar is that you can't see the scoreboard from it. You can see the game fine, for what that's worth, but if someone should hit a home run while you were down there you would miss the moment of supreme electronic ecstasy for which everyone waits. There you would be, stuck with a poorboy sandwich, while thirty or forty thousand people were experiencing a neon orgasm. Little wonder the place is empty most of the time.

My ticket entitled me to a red seat, the best that commoners can aspire to. I found the seat and whiled away the hour until game time by perusing a compendium called *Inside the Astrodome*. Reading it made me feel a little like Jonah probably felt when he was inside the whale. The book contained a letter from the President, another from the governor, a quote from Coleridge (guess which), a detailed comparison of the Astrodome and the Roman Colosseum, and page after page of staggering statistics. The stadium's iceplant, for example, can produce 36,000 pounds of ice a day—no one in this climate can fail to be impressed with such a figure.

The handbook also had a list of the fifty-three individually styled skyboxes which rim the top of the dome and which cost between $18,000 and $32,000 a season. There was the "River Shannon," the "Ramayana," and so on around the globe. After the game got under way, I counted the boxes with people in them and found that only twenty of the fifty-three were occupied. The man sitting next to me, a hearty, bearish fellow, didn't allow me to get any wrong ideas about the skyboxes, though. According to him the people who owned the other thirty-three were inside in the private apartments that go with each box, disporting themselves on the astrocouches (or astrobeds) and watching the game on closed-circuit TV.

"Yeah, that's where they are," the man said, yanking at his tie. He seemed like the sort of man who didn't wear a tie to work, but had put one on especially to come to the Astrodome. The thought that some wealthy lady might be copulating in a skybox clearly preyed on his mind.

I took his comment with a large grain of salt. The Texas middle class has always overestimated the sexuality of the Texas rich. Not many of the local rich would be inclined to make love at a ball game, even if they could manage it at that altitude. Later I learned that what they really do in the skyboxes is watch *Peyton Place*.

THE GAME THAT EVENING WAS between the Astros and the Mets, and it was obvious from the first pitch that most of the fans would not have bothered to sit through such a limp contest had it been taking place anywhere else. Even in the Dome, many of them might have left the game had it not been for the big electronic screen in centerfield. The game's true function was to provide material for the man who operated the screen. Whenever the Mets got a runner as far as second base the screen showed a foolhardy Met being smashed into the dust by a plummeting Astro, after which the word WHOA! appeared and the fans yelled WHOA! Usually this was sufficient to stop the Mets cold.

Later in the game, when the Astros unleashed the full fury of their normally inconspicuous attack, the screen assisted them on practically every pitch. When an Astro got on base there was a blast of heraldic trumpets and a little cavalryman (Teddy Roosevelt?) thundered across the screen, sabre raised. The word CHARGE! appeared, and the fans yelled CHARGE! Sometimes, instead of the cavalryman, a fierce little black bull came on and dashed about. When an Astro performed some particularly daring feat of base-running (like not quite getting picked off) the screen flashed OLE! and the fans yelled OLE! If the Astros push across two or three runs in one inning the trumpets and the charges and the bull and the cavalryman have the crowd in such a state of frenzy that the one thing they want to do is yell CHARGE! again.

It is fascinating to ponder the possible uses to which screen and scoreboard might be put. Billy Graham, for instance, finds the Dome a good place to crusade—but would a conversion be the equivalent of a home run or a single? When would one yell CHARGE? Or if the Dome were to be used for some social sport, like a political convention, wouldn't the man who controlled the screen control the convention?

On reflection, the comparison between the Dome and the Colosseum became a little disturbing. What but blood sport could ever be really violent enough for the Dome? When a gladiator fell, a huge thumb—turned down of course—could be flashed on the screen, followed by the words HOOK 'EM, HORNS! Texas fans could yell that with real enthusiasm.

After a while I got up and wandered back into the Upper Stands, to see how the game looked from there. Two old ladies sat just below me, one of them so armored with diamonds that she looked like some kind of eccentric crustacean. She ignored the game and kept her fieldglasses trained on one of the skyboxes. I gathered from the conversation that she owned the skybox, but had gone into temporary exile in the Upper Stands because her family had insisted on inviting guests she couldn't stand. She watched indignantly as the obnoxious someone made free with her liquor, and now and again, when the trumpets blared their command, she and her companion turned dutifully around and yelled CHARGE!

🐨

BY THE SEVENTH INNING THE screen had practically destroyed my will. Every time the trumpets sounded I felt the word "charge" forming on my lips. I got up and left, but after three hours in the Dome my sense of direction was in no better shape than my will, and I exited on the north side of the stadium, almost a mile from my car. At night, from the outside, the Dome looks very good, with the lights glowing through the roof and the white, serrated walls. I walked through the parking lot, down rows and rows and rows of cars, and after a while it dawned on me that all the cars were new—or nearly so. The parking lot was like a factory yard in Detroit. There was not a jalopy anywhere, just hundreds and hundreds of bright, rectangular rear ends, with now and then a fish-tail for variety. An affluent society indeed.

There were no kids outside the park, just cops and parking attendants, and I had a moment of nostalgia for the baseball I had watched as an adolescent, in good old Spudder Park, when Wichita Falls had a Class B franchise. If one got tired of seeing the Spudders get walloped it was only necessary to step outside the park to find some action. The grounds were alive with kids: Mexican, Negro, city kids, farm kids, all waiting hopefully for home-run balls or out-of-the-park foul tips. When one came over there was a scramble, and one grand night when the Spudders got walloped 30 to 1 our local nine garnered no less than seventeen practice balls. If no balls came over, the kids stood around under the liquid North Texas sky and swapped dirty jokes and bits of sexual folklore, a form of cultural exchange that benefitted us all.

I FOUND MY CAR WITH difficulty and drove away. It was clear then and is clearer now that the Astrodome would be an immense success, if for no other reason than that it itself is immense. Though it is a very pleasant place to watch a sports event, it is much more the product of a love of money and ostentation than of a love of sport. It caters quite successfully to what is least imaginative in the national character. Judge Roy Hofheinz, who masterminded the Dome, now intends to surround it with an eighteen-million-dollar amusement park and fourteen or fifteen million dollars' worth of motels, and these too, I imagine, will be immense successes, for his customers have more appetite for circuses than they now have for bread. (The Judge, by the way, is also *echt*-Texas. Those desiring elaboration are referred to page 57 of *You Be the Judge,* written by his daughter, Dene Hofheinz Mann. That page is a touchstone of a sort.)

A day or two after my visit to the Dome I heard that Boston was going to build one bigger than Houston's, and with a retractable roof besides. Atlanta has one in the offing, and no doubt others will follow; yet the prospect of being one-upped seems not to have agitated our civic bosom. Why should it? In Texas there is always room for something bigger. Soon some enterprising native will think of something new and even more extraordinary that Houston needs. Perhaps it will be a glassed-in aerial roadway from River Oaks to the Petroleum Club, or a mink Beatle wig to put over the Dome on cold days. Whatever it is will be bigger, better, sexier, more violent, and, above all, *costlier,* than anything we've had before. Houston is that kind of town.

A Handful of Roses

THE CITIES OF Texas, indeed, are that kind of cities, and it is not a point that need surprise anyone. The Anglos have only been in Texas about a hundred and fifty years, scarcely time enough for civilization to have had an appreciable spread. The Texan's primary concerns have been survival and exploitation: for the amenities there has been, until lately, little time to spare. As late as 1930 the state was still two-thirds rural. With the exception of San Antonio, our cities are all adolescent, and it is not surprising that they should seize the most obvious and most accessible symbols of prestige. Ripeness we simply do not have, nor do we value it much. The Texan may prefer his politicians a little oozy, but he likes his women green and his cities as raw as possible, so as to allow free play to what's left of the frontier spirit.

We are no longer so rustic, however, as to be above image-polishing. Size and cost may continue to be our primary considerations, but you won't hear us admitting it. Texans have finally learned that bragging is a form of discourse they can no longer afford. The sophisticated modern Texan will

not admit to size consciousness, or, indeed, to much of anything else. The old, loud, vulgar, groin-scratching Texan is
rapidly giving way to a quieter sort of citizen, one who
knows how to live with his itch. The new Texan tries for all
he's worth (and, frequently, *with* all he's worth) to be as
urbane as anybody else. The difficulty is that a genuinely
urban manner cannot be acquired in a day or even, perhaps,
in a generation, and that's as long as most Texans have been
working at it.

🦂

NOW THAT AIR TRAVEL HAS made it relatively easy to get in
and out of Texas, one tends to forget how interminable the
state once seemed. Size and distance impressed themselves
on visitors and native alike as something definitive. An
English friend once told me that until he crossed Texas by
car he had no real grasp of the concept of infinitude. We are
no longer the prisoners of distance, but I think it will be
awhile yet before we free ourselves of attitudes formed in
the days when we were creatures of the lonely plain and
knew nothing of streets and subdivisions. A just characterization of our cities must take account of the fact that many
of the people in them, and most of the people who control
them, remain, like Professor Webb, symbolic frontiersmen.
Wheelerdealerism is an extension of the frontier ethos,
refined and transplanted to an urban context; and while
only a few of us are wheeler-dealers, most of us practice
symbolic frontiersmanship in some form or fashion.

🦂

I DO, OF COURSE, WANT to be just to our cities. In Texas the
civic skin is very tender, and on the few occasions when I
have happened to prick it in the past, indignant readers have
hastened to remind me that there are plenty of cities in

America just as imperfect as Houston and Dallas. There are even, I am told, cities whose imperfections closely resemble those of Houston and Dallas, and I am quite prepared to believe that my readers are right. There probably are cities as tense as Dallas, as crass as Houston, as shallow as Austin. I don't doubt it. In all likelihood I have been in some of them. What I cannot imagine is why the existence of such imperfect cities should discourage me from writing frankly of Houston and Dallas. The assumption seems to be that because Pittsburgh is bad, Dallas should be spared all criticism. The implication that assumption but poorly conceals is that it is ungentlemanly to criticize homefolks when one could be criticizing outsiders. Where the failings of homefolk are concerned, a certain reticence is considered seemly.

Fortunately, such an attitude need not restrain us here. I would like to consider three cities only: Houston, Dallas, and Austin. For Texas they are quite clearly the style-changers, the cities which exert the strongest suction on the surrounding land. They are the maternity wards of urban Texas. Most of the other cities in the state are really only populous towns: one could live a lifetime in them and remain a country person. The pressures in Dallas and Houston can destroy or at least radically alter a rural orientation within a very few years.

San Antonio, of course, is a city. It is of Texas, and yet it transcends Texas in some way, as San Francisco transcends California, as New Orleans transcends Louisiana. Houston and Dallas express Texas—San Antonio speaks for itself, and much of its charm is in the way it embodies its past. Not a little of its charm, like that of El Paso, is attributable to the presence of Latins, who almost always improve an Anglo-Saxon town. For San Antonio's future, one has more fear than hope. HemisFair may prove an annunciation such as Yeats foresaw in "The Second Coming."

༅

THE SMALLER CITIES ARE CHARMING or not charming in direct proportion to their ratio of boosterism. Corpus Christi, El Paso, and Ft. Worth are all low-booster towns, and are, in their various ways, pleasant. The state contains a number of rather esoteric communities, of which Midland is perhaps the best example. Midland is a new oiltown, a community of some 70,000 nervous people located many many miles from anywhere amid the desolate West Texas plain. A few years ago it was said to have more millionaires per subdivision than any community in the country. Its unpleasantness quotient is very high; so high, in fact, that I have never been able to get a satisfactory count on the millionaires. The few I have met were so conservative as to be practically paralytic in social situations—next to rodeo cowboys they are the least communicative breed of people I have yet encountered. Mr. Bainbridge, hardened, no doubt, by years in New York, endured Midland long enough to get a good sampling of anecdotes, and the curious are referred to him.*

For the other cities—Waco, Beaumont, the oiltowns of East Texas (Lufkin, Longview, Tyler, Texarkana) and the triplets of the plains (Amarillo, Lubbock, Wichita Falls)—generosity asks a kind silence. There are people who love each and every one of them, it would seem. Indeed, so many people have responded belligerently to my castigations of Wichita Falls that I am moved to retreat a step or two in its favor. I once had a character say that it was the ugliest place on earth, but since that time extensive readings in the literature of Patagonia, Siberia and Central Asia have convinced me that, while dramatically apt, the statement should not be pressed as literally true. Ulan-Bator, Omsk, Semipalatinsk,

---

* *The SuperAmericans,* pp. 40–51.

Tashkent and some of the villages in the district of the Lob Nor, these are all at least as ugly, and doubtless the list will grow even longer as I read on.

AS I HAVE ALREADY SUGGESTED, a Quantity-Quality confusion is something most Texans have come by naturally. The pioneer Texan could hardly help thinking of life in terms of quantities; their descendants imbibed the concept of quantity with their mother's milk, had it fed into their vocabulary, and grew up to find it complexly entangled with their sense of self. "Best" is the superlative Texans usually tack onto those things they can allow themselves to be sentimental about (i.e. the best little woman, best damn horse, best little town), while "Biggest" is reserved for a more serious category (biggest ranch, biggest fortune, biggest failure, biggest deal).

Houston, our biggest city, thus falls naturally into the category of things to be taken seriously. It covers 440 square miles, has a population pushing a million and a half, and houses, as I have noted already, the phenomenal Astrodome, the state's most popular secular temple. The Dome, I think, may be the last great expression of the Old Vulgarity, and of the cherished Texas belief that if only one has enough money all fantasies are in reach. Money, like any other god, should be worshipped in a proper setting, and with an appropriate ritual, and the Dome provides both. If I have dwelt on it over-much, it is because it is a near-perfect symbol of Houston, a city with great wealth, some beauty, great energy, and all sorts of youthful confidence; but withal, a city that has not as yet had the imagination to match its money.

Houston has been a boom town for twenty years or more, and so far as one can tell the boom is still accelerating. Like

Los Angeles, it remains a city with no proper center, but is a loosely assembled collection of suburbs, districts, neighborhoods, some extremely luxurious, some extremely squalid. If one lives in River Oaks or in similarly lavish parts of town, munificence and reality begin to seem conterminous, and the squalors of the ghettos must appear to be no more than a terrible civic hallucination—as Watts must appear to the average resident of Beverly Hills. To examine such a city definitively one would have to fix an arbitrary center and move outward in narrow concentric circles until one reached the outermost shopping center or the last far-flung suburb—halfway to Galveston or a third of the way to Austin.

Fortunately, I had nothing that definitive in mind. As I said, Houston is a boom town, and boom towns do not differ all that much. Houston, like most of them, is lively, open, and violent. The common goal is tomorrow's dollar. Civic corruption is part of the game, and seldom draws more than a tolerant chuckle from the busy citizenry. The past yields to the present with a minimum of resistance. Indeed, unless the past can be sold it is summarily kicked out of the way. Let high-rise apartments really catch on and some imaginative entrepreneur will rent the San Jacinto monument and have it converted by Christmas. The arts are stolidly but dutifully supported, and there is the usual self-congratulatory talk about what a cultural center we have raised on the once-barren plain. The middle class are allowed to participate in the fantasies of the rich—a privilege they pay for eagerly—and the poor have the sufferings to which they are fairly accustomed, as the poet said.

Here, as in Los Angeles, many of the brightest, best-informed citizens have no roots in, interest in, or commitment to the community. If we have an equivalent to the movie industry it is the oil business, whose leading lights once got almost as much publicity as movie stars. Once, but no more. It is pretty clear that the day of the millionaire eccentric is over in Texas: our younger rich do their absolute best to behave like members of the middle class, and a great many of them succeed. The old were less self-conscious. Not long ago, in front of the Warwick Hotel (Houston's little acre of Beverly Hills) I actually heard a very wealthy, sixtyish lady order her chauffeur to pull her Cadillac alongside an acquaintance's Chrysler, so she could be sure her car was longer. The chauffeur did as commanded, and the lady, secure in her standards, surveyed the two vehicles with a critical eye, and when she was satisfied, waved the driver on. I felt as if I had probably seen the human equivalent of the last passenger pigeon.

If one were forced to choose a single aspect of Houston and from that aspect infer or characterize the city I think I would choose its bars, or, to be fully accurate, its bars and clubs. The upper class, for the most part, inhabits the upper air. Their clubs are very posh, if in a somewhat River Okie way, and tend to be altitudinally remote. There is a club on top of almost every tall building in town; the elevation they provide is both physical and psychological. They help relieve the hunger for heights that can seize one in a city only forty-one feet above sea level; and they also put their members well above the masses who cannot afford such relief.

The hundreds of middle-class clubs are generally squat one-story affairs, converted restaurants with imitation–Las Vegas furniture and deafening acoustics. They provide a certain relief from the neolithic Texas liquor laws and are rather rigidly divided as to clientele between "swinging singles" (their phrase) and uneasily marrieds who have just noticed middle age crooking his finger at them.

The poor have beer-bars, hundreds of them, seldom fancy

but reliably dim and cool. Most of them are equipped with jukeboxes, shuffleboards, jars of pig's feet and talkative drunks. There are lots of bar burlesques, where from 3 P.M. on girls gyrate at one's elbow with varying degrees of grace. On the east side there are a fair number of open air bars— those who like to watch the traffic can sit, drink Pearl, observe the wrecks, and listen to "Hello, Vietnam" on the jukebox. Louisiana is just down the road, and a lot of the men wear Cajun sideburns and leave their shirttails out. On the west side cowboys are common. Members of the cross-continental hitch-hiking set congregate on Franklin Street, at places like The Breaking Point Lounge. Symbolic *latinos* slip over to the Last Concert, on the north side; or, if they are especially bold, go all the way to McCarty Street, where one can view the most extraordinary example of Mexican saloon-and-whorehouse architecture north of the border.

My own sentimental favorite, the Angel Bar on Elysian Street, is now, alas, defunct; and I have never been able to find out if it went broke or if all the patrons killed themselves off. The waitress, a redheaded lady of advanced years, lushed happily all day on Thunderbird wine, and a jukebox full of wall-shaking Mexican music contrasted beautifully with a clientele of quietly menacing pachucos with tattoos on their fingers.

There is that characteristic disadvantage to the bars of Houston: they are among the best places in America to get killed. Compared to them, the Hell's Angels' hangouts in San Bernardino are havens of security. In May of 1966 I read, in the *Houston Post*, a homicide report that would have looked odd in any American daily except the *Houston Chronicle*. The killing took place in the Red Lilly Cafe, and since there was no sex interest the *Post*'s report was beautifully succinct:

Johnson's wife told police that the two men started argu-
ing about $45 that Hall allegedly owed Johnson. Both
men went for their guns and exchanged several shots,
police said.

Houston may be one of the last places left where men so
simply go for their guns when an argument gets hot. In 1966
a dozen such homicides were recorded in one weekend, a
record Tombstone or Dodge City would have been hard put
to match even in their heydays. A few months ago an editor
of my acquaintance came to Houston for the night.
Somewhere between the airport and town he stopped at a
bar to wet his whistle, and while doing that he called me.
We had hardly got past the formalities when his voice was
drowned out by a chorus of shrieks, the sound of breaking
glass, and the report of a gun. "Christ," he said, "they're
fighting in here. I've got to get out." He hurried away without hanging up the phone, and I listened to the shrieks for a
while. His name was not in next morning's homicide
columns, so I assume he made it to safety.

One cannot help believing that Houston's astonishing
homicide rate is related to its equally astonishing rate of
growth. A great many Houstonians are still in the process of
transition from country ways to city ways. They are not yet
urban, but they are no longer quite country, either. Many of
them are poor, and the unaccustomed urban pressures frus-
trate them severely. To let off steam they go to honky-
tonks—dance-halls for country people who are no longer in
the country. The honky-tonk jukeboxes are full of country
music, a music that sustains its patrons' nostalgia for an
Edenic rural past. In such a place, with a little beer under
his belt, a man is apt to find that his frustrations are uncon-
tainable: he has more steam to let off than he had realized,

and he may let it off by shooting some poor bastard whose plight is little different from his own.

The murders are triggered by the most trivial irritations: last year a man was shot because he refused to lend another a nickel, and, more recently still, a gun-toter threw down on a waiter and shot him dead because there were too few beans in his chili. A few years ago a countryman, bewildered to the point of dementia, stabbed his wife to death in the parking lot of a hospital, all the while singing "Jesus, Lover of My Soul." There is one amazing bar where the customers apparently congregate for the express purpose of showing off their guns, although most of the weapons exhibited are of the cheapest sort, ten- and fifteen-dollar pistols which are barely accurate the length of the bar. Of course, they are rarely fired at anything (or anyone) farther away than that. The mere possession of a gun often serves to bolster up the shaky confidence of a city-billy who has not yet learned to handle himself in the city.

✺

IT IS NOT, OF COURSE, that there are *no* urbane people in Houston. Until recently they were so scattered and in such a minority that their presence scarcely seemed to affect the city's character, but this is changing and their numbers are increasing rapidly. Houston is easily the most female city in Texas, and the next quarter-century will probably decide what kind of woman she will be. She may become a penny-clutching widower, or she may, with her money and her sexy trees, attract and accept the sort of imagination that could bring her to a rich maturity and make her a mother city. Even now she is being fecundated by a diversity of peoples, and her children might be interesting to know. They will be natural urbanites, most of them, members of the first generation of Texans to belong in fact and in spirit to a fertile city, not to the Old Man of the country or the Old Maid of the towns.

⁊

DALLAS IS MORE LIKE HOUSTON than either city would readily admit, but there are a few crucial differences: Houston doesn't mind being thought a boom town; it feels damn good about itself and tends to be completely convinced by its own publicity. Houstonians are secure to the point of smugness about their city: they expect people to like it (and them) and are amazed and perplexed when someone doesn't.

Not so Dallas. It is one of the uneasiest cities in the country, and was that way long before the assassination. Well-to-do Houstonians are not only convinced that they are valuable, they are convinced they are wonderful. Well-to-do Dallasans regard themselves with considerable less certainty. They are tentative, not quite sure who they are supposed to be, not really confident that who they are supposed to be is worth being. It is, consequently, the city of the instant put-down, and the higher one goes in the Dallas establishment the more true this is likely to be. Nowhere else in the state does one find so many bitter, defensive, basically insecure people in positions of power.

What well-to-do Dallasans *are* very often convinced of is that they are right. The Kennedy assassination and the Johnson presidency made self-questioners of many Texans, but the citizens of Dallas, now that the city's economy has survived the assassination, seem almost as self-righteous as ever. Indeed, part of the civic unease may be a result of the city's own very effective publicity. Dallas was the first Texas city to publicize itself heavily as a center of culture and sophistication, a campaign which seems to have contributed to the confusion of the populace. Such sophistication and culture as Dallas has is mostly hybrid, not indigenous. Like Houston, it is a business town, and always has been. For a generation or so its more affluent children have been provided with Eastern educations, and those of them who return to Dallas have to work at culture like mad to keep from feeling they are wasting themselves. The citizens of Dallas have the strain of maintaining the delusion that in their city culture, not money, counts most. As in Houston, wealth and ostentation are respected, even adored, while art is dutifully (and on the whole, crudely) patronized. Art is not really as important as money, but it is nonetheless something to be taken Very Seriously. The eccentric is not welcomed; the patrons are not confident enough to be comfortable in the presence of someone radically unlike themselves.

A year or so ago, for example, the energetic young novelist and psychedeliust Ken Kesey flew into Dallas for a Book-and-Author affair. Mr. Kesey responds very acutely to his surroundings, and after a day or two of Dallas parties, where tensions and hostilities flicker like prairie lightning, he decided that the way to survive Dallas would be to get above it. Accordingly, he got high and stayed high, and, just before his speech, took the further precaution of supplying himself with a bag full of red rubber balls. His speeches tend to be loosely extemporized, and this one, I judge, was no exception. He was only getting plane fare for his trouble, and had felt under no obligation to write anything. Now and then, as he spoke, he threw the red rubber balls at what he judged to be hostile faces in the crowd, a tactic which disconcerted his audience and left his sponsors highly dismayed. It was clearly no way to approach High Culture. Upon consultation, the sponsors decided that such irregularity ought to be punished, so they withheld the plane fare and told Mr. Kesey he could get back to California as best he could. He responded by threatening to invade a Murchison party, where he proposed to scrounge ticket-money from the guests. The thought of such an indecorous proceedings had the desired effect, and the sponsors grudgingly forked over.

❦

OTHERWISE, MOST OF WHAT I have said about Houston and Houston's pretensions could simply be repeated for Dallas. Houston is open, an opportunist's delight. Dallas is cleaner than Houston: cleaner because more tightly controlled. In Dallas the ruling oligarchy is old, cagey, and so well-entrenched as to be practically invulnerable to rude invasion. The newspapers in both cities are languid and establishmentarian, but politically Dallas is the more extreme. The savagery of its perfervid conservatives is so well known that most politicians now give the town a wide berth.

This conservatism is compounded of fear and boredom and in tone closely resembles religious hysteria. In Dallas a flavorless Protestantism seems to have yielded super-patriotism as by-product. The Dallas true believers have made conservatism a religion-surrogate: they hate liberals the way passionate religious dogmatists once hated heretics. Orthodoxy is the American way of life as lived in Highland Park, and Earl Warren, among others, should be sent to the stake. Indeed, J. Evetts Haley drew wild applause in Dallas for suggesting that Warren should be hanged.

The city contains one of the more picturesque skid rows in the state, a section known as Deep Ellum. There is a glossy picture of Jack Ruby in the window of a pawn shop there—a picture taken in his glossy days, such as they were. His head is enfolded between the breasts of one of his strippers. Nearby, apropos of nothing, is a yellowing newspaper picture of the Kennedy brothers, and nearby that a photograph of the bullet-riddled body of some gangster, Dillinger or Pretty Boy Floyd or perhaps Clyde Barrow, whose grave is across the Trinity in Oak Cliff. A few windows away there is, or used to be, a shiny nickel-plated submachine gun, of the type Bonnie and Clyde were said to use. And if one walks west along Pawn Shop Row, past windows full of pistols and ankle-knives with twelve-inch blades, one comes in a few blocks to the junction of Elm and Ervay and can turn north and see the famous gold-bannistered staircase in the lobby of the Republic National Bank.

Wealth, violence, and poverty are common throughout Texas, and why the combination should be scarier in Dallas than elsewhere I don't know. But it is: no place in Texas is quite so tense and so tight. Violence in Houston is extremely common, but there it lies close to the surface and is easily predicted and fairly easily avoided. Dallas is a city of underground men: the violence there lies deeper, and is under greater pressure. It may not surface for a long time, but when it does, as we all know, it surfaces like Spindletop.

🐨

WE CAN AT LEAST BE thankful that underground men are difficult to organize. If Dallas could accomplish that, who knows what would happen? They might come to Houston and take away our Astrodome; or they might, on the other hand, rush down to Austin and secure themselves a sniper's nest from which to defend themselves against the armies of the Mistaken (*Life Line*'s term) who want to take their goods and privileges and give them to Negroes and Communists. In such an event they would choose, of course, the famous eighteen-story shaft on the University of Texas campus, a structure that, long before the Whitman tragedy, had attracted the deranged among us—though usually only for the purpose of self-destruction.

In Houston and Dallas the many tall buildings tend to neutralize one another, but the Tower easily dominates the landscape of Austin, its only rival being the Dome of the capitol. The Tower houses the should-be intellectuals who administer the University; the Dome the all-too-genuine politicians who run the state. Betwixt this twain lie the gaming fields of Austin, so fertile with schizophrenia—a gay and crowded social greensward where Knowledge courts Power, and where the intellectual gourmet and the sexual gourmand sometimes feast together on the same rump.

Austin is a happy place, sort of; foreigners and easterners surrender their affections to Austin more readily than to any other place in the state. They come reluctantly, drawn by the fragrance of our cash, and a great many of them stay. It is a pretty, sunny town, the climate warm, the sky blue and unsmogged. The sun sets plangent and golden into the purple of the Austin hills at evening, and the moon, whiter than a breast, lights the Colorado River. The students, those darlings, return year after year like the swans of Yeats, unwearied by passion or conquest, young, clean, beautifully limbed, and, as often as not, innocently promiscuous. If, for some reason, the students fail to gather at one's bed, there are certain to be Wives, legislative, academic, or miscellaneous, some of them long in the tooth and lean in the shank, others graceful and nervous as does, but all of them, it sometimes seems, dedicated to the principle that the horn is always greener on the other guy.*

Year after year literary celebrities descend on Austin, and, one by one, year after year, the Wives ambush them at the first bend in the party and hasten them off to bed. The results have been known to make sexual pessimists of both Wives and celebrities, but they also provide the indispens-

---

* I am indebted to Ken Kesey for the phrasing of this principle. He got it, I believe, from a teeny-bopper.

able raw material for the Southwest's most productive gossip mill.

🪳

MY OWN PERIOD OF RESIDENCE in Austin was blessedly short. I lived there for eight months in 1963, and I feel no impulse to write at length about the city since there exists a lively and accurate book about it, William Brammer's *The Gay Place*. Mr. Dobie, Mr. Bedichek, and Dr. Webb lived in Austin for many years, but the city never became their spiritual property to the extent to which it is now the spiritual property of Mr. Brammer. How he may eventually improve the property we must wait to discover, but I am of the opinion that his slow-growing second novel *Fustian Days* will treat the Austin of the sixties as well as *The Gay Place* treated the Austin of the fifties.

During the last two months of my stay in Austin it was my good fortune to be thrown much in the company of Mr. Brammer. We were both, at the time, in respite of wives and money, and shared a house on Windsor Road. Mr. Brammer was at that time the local culture hero, *The Gay Place* having been published only two years before. He was thus a natural target for anyone in Austin who was aspiring, frustrated, or bored. The inrush of Wives threatened to wrench the hinges off the door, and Mr. Brammer faced it with the courteous and rather melancholy patience with which he would probably face a buffalo stampede. In the wake of the Wives came a sweaty and verbally diarrhetic mass of bored or bitter professors, broke or bitter politicians, proto-hippies with beach balls full of laughing gas, and broke-bored-bitter young journalists who looked like they had been using themselves for blotters.

In time I sealed off my part of the house and left Bill to cope with the crowd as best he could, but during the brief weeks when I spent my nights opening the door I got, it seemed to me, an adequate glimpse of Austin. It had, among other adolescent characteristics, a fascination with its own pubic hair, and a corresponding uneasy fear that its sexual development might stop just short of adequacy. Groupiness was endemic. No one might be missing from the group, lest he turn out to be somewhere better, with a wilder, more swinging group. In such a town the person who is sure of himself is apt to be literally crushed by the surging mobs of the insecure, all rushing to confirm themselves by association.

I am told that my view of Austin is too limited, that higher on the slopes, in secluded dells, the significant political and intellectual work of Austin goes on, serious, responsible, mature. Maybe, and again, maybe not. There are indeed a fair number of first-rate people on the faculty of the University, but for the most part these are all people whose accomplishment guarantees them the freedom to leave Austin frequently—a freedom most of them take full advantage of. Habitance there is occasionally convenient for them, but they scarcely alter the tone of the community. Indeed, it could even be argued that Austin has begun to work against them intellectually by encouraging them to think of themselves as a group.

Cliquishness can be especially insidious in a town the size of Austin, where those in favor seldom if ever receive any strong-minded local criticism. This same factor, as I have said, worked against Dobie and Webb and Bedichek.

ॐ

THE EMOTIONAL ACTIVITY MOST CHARACTERISTIC of Austin is, I think, the attempt to acquire power through knowledge. Accordingly, Austin is the one town in the state where there is a real tolerance of the intellectual; and yet one's final impression of Austin is of widespread intellectual confusion. Perhaps the phenomenon most expressive of this paradox is the University's rare book program. For the last decade, rare books have been sucked into Austin like particles of dust into a vacuum cleaner; the University's enormous and almost amorphous acquisitiveness remains the wonder, joy, and despair of the rare book world. No one can doubt that an extraordinary library is being formed in Austin, one whose potential usefulness is very great; yet the manner in which it is being formed leaves one a trifle abashed. The Humanities Research Center, for all its riches, comes too close to being a kind of intellectual's Astrodome. The University's almost frenzied acquisitiveness seems to stem not so much from a vision of the needs of future generations as from its own immediate intellectual insecurity. A successful acquisition brings a temporary sense of intellectual power, and it is the acquisition of books and manuscripts, rather than their use, which seems to be the dominant concern; that and the creation of a symbol of prestige (the Center) which the scholarly world cannot ignore.

꽃

THIS MEGALOMANIACAL ACQUISITION OF BOOKS, like the equally megalomaniacal boosterism which afflicts almost all our cities, might serve as a reminder that in an assessment of Austin (or Texas) there is yet a greater megalomaniac to be considered. Austin is Johnson's town, and before long the king will be returning to the counting house. What he will do there is not, at the moment, an especially fruitful subject for speculation, but it will not be likely to decrease the insecurity of Austin's intellectual community. Austin intellectuals have always been frightened and awed by Johnson's force, and, though the imagery differs, they accord him the sort of respect that Milton accorded Satan.

MOST OF WHAT I HAVE HAD to say about the cities of Texas is embarrassingly obvious. They are young, boosteristic, and very hot for the Big Buck. I could blow the present chapter to three times this length with a few lungsful of local color, but that would not alter the theme. It might be more profitable to speculate for a moment upon the relationship of Texas writers to their cities. It occurred to me recently that if I were to set a novel in Austin I would very likely model my heroine after a certain young lady. Like Mr. Brammer, she was for years one of the guardian spirits of Austin, and, like Mr. Brammer, she has now gone elsewhere. She is to Austin and the generation of the New Disorder in Texas as Neal Cassady was to Denver and the Beats, a reflection sufficient in itself to convince me I have no business setting a novel in Austin. Seldom does the impulse to apotheosize or exploit a given human model produce a truly resonant novel.

I doubt, in fact, that I have any business setting a novel in any city, Texan or otherwise, for though I have lived in cities twelve years they have apparently failed to seed my imagination with those pregnant images from which a living and well-voiced fiction might grow. In this I seem to be one with my regional contemporaries; with very few exceptions, no Texas novelist has drawn a novel of any distinction out of city experience.

This of course is a circumstance sure to be altered soon. For the moment, however, the point stands: we are country writers yet, but country writers who have moved to the city to write. We are several degrees more remote from the country than Bedichek or Dobie, but the emotions, images, symbols that animate our books pertain to the country still. We too are symbolic frontiersmen, most of us, attempting to keep the frontiersman's sense of daring and independence by seeking these qualities, not in the life of action but in the life of the mind. It is still daring enough, in Texas, to commit oneself to the life of the mind, and it is our only corollary to that other kind of daring—a kind that has small place in this land of cities.

If this is true, our choice of forms may be of some interest. Our predecessors, those men of the country, all chose nonfiction, but nowadays the drift is definitely toward the novel. Something like seventeen novels were published last year by Texans. Probably a hundred novels a year get written in Texas now, and a good many of them get published. As living gets easier and more circumscribed, the imagination pushes farther and farther, replacing the open range with open forms.

One of my covert purposes in writing this book was to find out for myself if nonfiction could be as interesting and as rich a mode as fiction. After all, a great many talented people have diverted more and more of their energies to nonfiction within the last decade—enough to make one curious. Why Mr. Mailer, Mr. Baldwin, Miss McCarthy, Mr. Capote, Mr. Vidal and others of their generation are so often more persuasive in their essays than in their novels is of course a subtle question; possibly it is a delayed result of the contempt for narrative fostered by modernist literary theory. Or possibly it is because the problem of cliche has recently become more acute. Black humour seemed to offer a solution to the problem of cliche, but it is clearly not one that will remain viable very long. In any case, with narrative in fiction gone out of fashion we might expect the narrative sense either to atrophy or to be diverted, and the latter, it seems to me, is what has happened. The narrative impulse has been diverted. Many of the great essays of the last decade are essays in which both the tactics and the textures of fiction have been assimilated.

Be that as it may, I was not long in discovering that it wasn't going to work for me. I had rather write straight fictions than pseudo-fictions (the term is not meant to be pejorative), and my preference for the straight fiction is principally a matter of voice. However well-pitched, clever, or sincere, my voice in the essay counts for much less than the voice of the novel. It is not a question of monotony, but of range and resonance and fullness, and on all three counts the novel outspeaks.

To put it in imagery more appropriate to my immediate subject; nonfiction is a pleasant way to walk, but the novel puts one horseback, and what cowboy, symbolic or real, would walk when he could ride? In the novel, as in riding, there is the sense that one's own speed is increased, one's movement supported and enlarged by the speed and movement of another life; and for me the motion of a novel is far more satisfying than the fidgetings of the brain that produce nonfiction. This sense of another life is not quite so romantic or anti-intellectual as it might seem, for the novel still depends upon the creation of character, an element in fiction about as unfashionable as narrative and fully as important. I do not say that narrative and character should be stressed at the expense of structure and symbol, but merely that the former are much more important than the poetics of fiction has made them seem.

<hr />

WHEN MY FATHER WAS TWELVE MY grandfather sent him, alone, with a small herd of steers, to Graham, Texas, a town about forty miles from our ranch. He was to sell the steers, buy new cattle, drive them home, and show a profit—all of which, from all reports, he did. At twelve I would have been hard put to drive a very docile herd of steers forty yards, but at twelve I did discover *Don Quixote*. I was permanently altered by it, and just in time, too. Even if I could have driven a herd of steers to Graham I should have had to cut a hundred fences to get there, or else open a hundred gates.

In their youth, as I have said, my uncles sat on the barn and watched the last trail herds moving north—I sat on the self-same barn and saw only a few oil-field pickups and a couple of dairy trucks go by. That life died, and I am lucky to have found so satisfying a replacement as *Don Quixote* offered. And yet, that first life has not quite died in me—not quite. I missed it only by the width of a generation and, as I was growing up, heard the whistle of its departure. Not long after I entered the pastures of the empty page I realized that the place where all my stories start is the heart faced suddenly with the loss of its country, its customary and legendary range.

That loss brings me to my final chapter. My generation had the country only long enough to realize that something was going, but with my father and my uncles it was different: they were of the last generation of Texans to have it fully. The country was the ground of their life, their womb, their daylight, and their tomb, and one might now properly ask to whom they have left that country: myself, or Hud?

The question, I realize, is slightly misleading, for it is clear that despite themselves they left their country to the suburbanized middle class, whom they would have held in large contempt. It is possible, though, that what they left was a split legacy, one that may gain them a sort of symbolic revenge on their unwitting heirs. The middle class will get the land, one way or another, but Hud and I were left the water rights. That is, we were left the mythology, he to live it and I to dramatize it. In the final chapter I should like to consider how that mythology operated in the lives of some of my blood kinsmen, and how, by extension, it is operating now in my own books and the books of my artistic kinsmen.

Take My Saddle from the Wall: A Valediction

Stranger: "Mr. Goodnight, you have been a man of
vision."
Charles Goodnight: "Yes, a hell of a vision."
                                    —J. Frank Dobie, Cow People

Oh, when I die take my saddle from the wall,
Put it on my pony, lead him from the stall,
Tie my bones to his back, turn our faces to the West,
And we'll ride the prairie that we love the best . . .
                                    —"Goodbye, Old Paint"

FOR BRAIDING I have no gift. During the time when I was
nominally a cowboy I would sometimes try to braid a halter,
a rope, or a bridle rein, usually with sad results. I could seldom make the strands I worked with lay easily or neatly
together; and so it may be, I fear, with the braid of this book.

The reader who has attended thus far will have noticed a
certain inconsistency in my treatment of Texas past and
present—a contradiction of attractions, one might call it. I
am critical of the past, yet apparently attracted to it; and
though I am even more critical of the present I am also
quite clearly attracted to *it*. Such contradictions are always a
bit awkward to work with, but in this case there is even an
added difficulty: the strands of subject which I have
attempted to braid are not of equal width, and I have only

managed to twist them into a very rough plait. That I have not been able to do a smoother job is probably due to the fact that I am a novelist, and thus quite unaccustomed to the strain of prolonged thought. My first concern has commonly been with textures, not structures; with motions, rather than methods. What in this book appear to be inconsistencies of attitude are the manifestations of my ambivalence in regard to Texas—and a very deep ambivalence it is, as deep as the bone. Such ambivalence is not helpful in a discursive book, but it can be the very blood of a novel.

I realize that in closing with the McMurtrys I may only succeed in twisting a final, awkward knot into this uneven braid, for they bespeak the region—indeed, are eloquent of it—and I am quite as often split in my feelings about them as I am in my feelings about Texas. They pertain, of course, both to the Old Texas and the New, but I choose them here particularly because of another pertinence. All of them gave such religious allegiance as they had to give to that god I mentioned in my introduction: the god whose principal myth was the myth of the Cowboy, the ground of whose divinity was the Range. They were many things, the McMurtrys, but to themselves they were cowboys first and last, and the rituals of that faith they strictly kept.

Now the god has departed, thousands of old cowboys in his train. Among them went most of the McMurtrys, and in a few more years the tail-end of the train will pass from sight. All of them lived to see the ideals of the faith degenerate, the rituals fall from use, the principal myth become corrupt. In my youth, when they were old men, I often heard them yearn aloud for the days when the rituals had all their power, when they themselves had enacted the pure, the original myth, and I know that they found it bitter to leave the land to which they were always faithful to the strange and godless heirs that they had bred. I write of them here not to pay them homage, for the kind of homage I could pay they would neither want nor understand; but as a gesture of recognition, a wave such as riders sometimes give one another as they start down opposite sides of a hill. The kind of recognition I would hope to achieve is a kind that kinsmen are so frequently only able to make in a time of parting.

☙

I HAVE NEVER CONSIDERED GENEALOGY much of an aid to recognition, and thus have never pursued my lineage any distance at all. I remember my McMurtry grandparents only dimly, and in very slight detail, and only a few of the many stories I have heard about them strike me as generative. My grandfather, William Jefferson McMurtry, was the first man I ever saw who wore a mustache—a heavy grey one—and when I think of him I think first of that mustache. He died when I was four and only three stories about him have stuck in my mind.

The first was that he was a drunkard in his middle age, and that my grandmother, burdened with many children and unburdened by any conveniences, had found his drunkenness tiresome and threatened to leave him if he didn't stop drinking. The threat was undoubtedly made in earnest, and he took it so immediately to heart that he stopped drinking then and there, with a jug half-full of whiskey hanging in the saddle room of the barn. The jug of whiskey hung untouched for nineteen years, until the nail rusted out and it fell.

I remember, too, that it was said he could stand on the back porch of the ranch-house and give a dinner call that his boys could hear plainly in the lower field, two miles away. As a boy, riding across the lower field, I would sometimes look back at the speck of the ranch-house and imagine that I heard the old man's dinner call carrying across the flats.

My grandmother's name was Louisa Francis. By the time I was old enough to turn outward, she had turned inward and was deaf, chair-bound, and dying. She lived until I was nine, but I cannot recall that we ever communicated. She was a small woman, wizened by hardship, and I thought her very stern. One day when I was in my teens I went down the crude stone steps to the spring that had been for years the family's only source of water, and it occurred to me that carrying water up those steps year after year would make a lady stern. The children all spoke of William Jefferson as if they had liked him and got on with him well enough, but they spoke of Lousia Francis as one speaks of the Power. I have since thought that an element in her sternness might have been a grim, old-lady recognition that the ideal of the family was in the end a bitter joke; for she had struggled and kept one together, and now, after all, they had grown and gone and left her, and in that hard country what was there to do but rock to death?

William Jefferson, however, sustained himself well to the end, mostly I judge, on inquisitiveness. Since eleven of the twelve children were gone, my father bore the brunt of this inquisitiveness, and one can imagine that it became oppressive at times. When my father returned to the ranch late at night from a trip or a dance the old man would invariably hear his car cross the rattly cattleguard and would hasten out in the darkness to get the news, as it were. Generally the two would meet halfway between the barn and the backyard gate, William Jefferson fresh with queries and midnight speculations on the weather or this or that, my father— mindful that the morning chores were just over the hill— anxious to get to bed. By the time Grandfather died the habit had grown so strong that three years passed before my father could walk at night from the barn to the backyard gate without encountering the ghost of William Jefferson somewhere near the chicken house.

❦

PIONEERS DIDN'T HASTEN TO WEST Texas like they hastened to the southern and eastern parts of the state. At first
glance, the region seemed neither safe nor desirable;
indeed, it wasn't safe, and it took the developing cattle
industry to render it desirable. My grandparents arrived in
1877 and prudently paused for ten years in Denton
County, some sixty miles west of Dallas and not quite on
the lip of the plains. The fearsome Comanche had been
but recently subdued—in fact, it was still too early to tell
whether they *were* subdued. The last battle of Adobe Walls
was fought in the Panhandle in 1874, and Quanah Parker
surrendered himself and his warriors in 1875. The very next
year, sensing a power vacuum, Charles Goodnight drove
his herds into the Palo Duro; Satanta, the last great war
chief of the Kiowa, killed himself in prison in 1878.
Remnants of the two nations trickled into the reservation
for the next few years; there were occasional minor hostilities on the South Plains as late as 1879. The Northern
Cheyenne broke out in 1878—who could be sure the
Comanches wouldn't follow their example? To those
brought up on tales of Comanche terror the psychological
barrier did not immediately fall. The Comanche never
committed themselves readily to the reservation concept,
and for a time there remained the chance that one might
awaken in the night in that lonely country to find oneself
and one's family being butchered by a few pitiless, reac-
tionary warriors bent on a minor hostility.

At any rate, in the eighties William Jefferson and Louisa
Francis and their first six children moved a hundred miles
farther west, to Archer County, where, for three dollars an
acre, they purchased a half-section of land. They settled near
a good seeping spring, one of the favorite watering places on
a military road that then ran from Fort Belknap to Buffalo

Springs. The forts that the road connected soon fell from use, but cattle drivers continued to use the trail and the spring for many years. The young McMurtry boys had only to step out their door to see their hero figures riding past.

Indeed, from the pictures I have seen of the original house, they could have ignored the door altogether and squeezed through one of the walls. Life in such a house, in such a country, must surely have presented formidable difficulties, and the boys (there were eventually nine, as against three girls) quite sensibly left home as soon as they had mastered their directions.

The median age for leave-taking seems to have been seventeen, and the fact that the surrounding country was rapidly filling up with farmers merely served as an added incentive to departure. The cowboy and the farmer are genuinely inimical types: they have seldom mixed easily. To the McMurtrys, the plow and the cotton-patch symbolized not only tasks they loathed but an orientation toward the earth and, by extension, a quality of soul which most of them not-so-covertly despised. A "one-gallus farmer" ranked very low in their esteem, and there were even McMurtrys who would champion the company of Negroes and Mexicans over the company of farmers—particularly if the farmers happened to be German. The land just to the north of the McMurtry holdings was settled by an industrious colony of German dairymen, and the Dutchmen (as they were called) were thought to be a ridiculous and unsightly thorn in the fair flesh of the range.

In later years two or three of the McMurtry brothers increased their fortunes through farming, but this was a fact one seldom heard bruited about. Indeed, I heard no discussion of the matter until fairly recently, when one of the farms sold for an even million dollars, a figure capable of removing the blight from almost any scutcheon.

꿎

THE COWBOY'S CONTEMPT OF THE farmer was not unmixed with pity. The farmer walked in the dust all his life, a hard and ignominious fate. Cowboys could perform terrible labors and endure bone-grinding hardships and yet consider themselves the chosen of the earth; and the grace that redeemed it all in their own estimation was the fact that they had gone a-horseback. They were riders, first and last. I have known cowboys broken in body and twisted in spirit, bruised by debt, failure, loneliness, disease and most of the other afflictions of man, but I have seldom known one who did not consider himself phenomenally blessed to have been a cowboy, or one who could not cancel half the miseries of existence by dwelling on the horses he had ridden, the comrades he had ridden them with, and the manly times he had had. If the cowboy is a tragic figure, he is certainly one who will not accept the tragic view. Instead, he helps his delineators wring pathos out of tragedy by ameliorating his own loss into the heroic myth of the horseman.

To be a cowboy meant, first of all, to be a horseman. Mr. Dobie was quite right when he pointed out that the seat of the cowboy's manhood is the saddle. I imagine, too, that he understood the consequences of that fact for most cowboys and their women, but if so he was too kindly a man to spell out the consequences in his books. I would not wish to make the point crudely, but I do find it possible to doubt that I have ever known a cowboy who liked women as well as he liked horses, and I know that I have never known a cowboy who was as comfortable in the company of women as he was in the company of his fellow cowboys.

I pointed out in Chapter 4 that I did not believe this was the result of repressed homosexuality, but of a commitment to a heroic concept of life that simply takes little account of women. Certainly the myth of the cowboy is a very efficacious myth, one based first of all upon a deep response to nature. Riding out at sunup with a group of cowboys, I have often felt the power of that myth myself. The horses pick their way delicately through the dewy country, the brightness of sunrise has not yet fallen from the air, the sky is blue and all-covering, and the cowboys are full of jokes and morning ribaldries. It is a fine action, compelling in itself and suggestive beyond itself of other centuries and other horsemen who have ridden the earth.

Unfortunately, the social structure of which that action is a part began to collapse almost a hundred years ago, and the day of the cowboy is now well into its evening. Commitment to the myth today carries with it a terrible emotional price—very often the cowboy becomes a victim of his own ritual. His women, too, are victims, though for the most part acquiescent victims. They usually buy the myth of cowboying and the ideal of manhood it involves, even though both exclude them. A few even buy it to the point of attempting to assimilate the all-valuable masculine qualities to themselves, producing that awful phenomenon, the cowgirl.

If, as I suggested earlier, the cowboy is a tragic figure, one element of the tragedy is that he is committed to an orientation that includes but does not recognize the female, which produces, in day-to-day life, an extraordinary range of frustrations. Curiously, the form the cowboy's recognition does take is literary: he handles women through a romantic convention. The view is often proffered by worshippers of the cowboy that he is a realist of the first order, but that view is an extravagant and imperceptive fiction. Cowboys are romantics, extreme romantics, and ninety-nine out of a hundred of them are sentimental to the core. They are oriented toward the past and face the present only under duress, and then with extreme reluctance.

People who think cowboys are realists generally think so because the cowboy's speech is salty and apparently straight-forward, replete with the wisdom of natural men. What that generally means is that cowboy talk sounds shrewd and perceptive, and so it does. In fact, however, both the effect and the intention of much cowboy talk is literary: cowboys are aphorists. Whenever possible, they turn their observations into aphorisms. Some are brilliant aphorists, scarcely inferior to Wilde or La Rochefoucauld; one is proud to steal from them. I plucked a nice one several years ago, to wit: "A woman's love is like the morning dew: it's just as apt to fall on a horseturd as it is on a rose." In such a remark the phrasing is worth more than the perception, and I think the same might be said for the realism of most cowboys. It is a realism in tone only: its insights are either wildly romantic, mock-cynical, or solemnly sentimental. The average cowboy is an excellent judge of horseflesh, only a fair judge of men, and a terrible judge of women, particularly "good women." Teddy Blue state it succinctly forty years ago:

> I'd been traveling and moving around all the time and I can't say I ever went out of my way to seek the company of respectable ladies. We (cowboys) didn't consider we were fit to associate with them on account of the company we kept. We didn't know how to talk to them anyhow. That was what I meant by saying the cowpunchers was afraid of a decent woman. We were so damned scared that we'd do or say something wrong . . .*

That was written of the nineteenth century cowboy, but it would hold good for most of their descendants, right down

---

* *We Pointed Them North*, p. 188.

to now. Most of them marry, and love their wives sincerely, but since their sociology idealizes women and their mythology excludes her, the impasse which results is often little short of tragic. Now, as then, the cowboy escapes to the horse, the range, the work, and the company of comrades, most of whom are in the same unacknowledged fix.

Once more I might repeat what cannot be stressed too often: that the master symbol for handling the cowboy is the symbol of the horseman.* The gunman had his place in the mythology of the West, but the cowboy did not realize himself with a gun. Neither did he realize himself with a penis, nor with a bankroll. Movies fault the myth when they dramatize gunfighting, rather than horsemanship, as the dominant skill. The cowboy realized himself on a horse, and a man might be broke, impotent, and a poor shot and still hold up his head if he could ride.

❦

HOLDING UP THE HEAD HAD its importance too, for with horsemanship went pride, and with that, stoicism. The cowboy, like Mithridates, survived by preparing for ill and not for good—after all, it sometimes took only a prairie-dog hole to bring a man down. Where emotion was concerned, the cowboy's ethic was Roman: emotion, but always emotion within measure. A uncle of mine put it as nicely as one could want. This one was no McMurtry, but an uncle-by-

---

* *Singing Cowboy,* ed. Margaret Larkin, Oak Publications, New York, 1963, p. 60. See in this regard the well-known song "My Love Is a Rider," a song said to have been composed by Belle Starr: *He made me some presents among them a ring. The return that I made him was a far better thing. 'Twas a young maiden's heart I would have you all know, He won it by riding his bucking bronco. Now listen young maidens where e're you reside, Don't list to the cowboy who swings the rawhide. He'll court you and pet you and leave you and go Up the trail in the spring on his bucking bronco.*

marriage named Jeff Dobbs. He had been a cowboy and a Texas Ranger, and when he had had enough of the great world he retired to the backwoods of Oklahoma to farm peanuts and meditate on the Gospels. He was a self-styled Primitive Baptist, which meant that he had a theology all his own, and he had honed his scriptural knife to a fine edge in some forty years of nightly arguments with his wife, my Aunt Minta. Neither of them ever yielded a point, and when my aunt was killed I don't think they even agreed on the book of Zechariah.

One morning not unlike any other, Aunt Minta went out in her car, was hit by a truck, and killed instantly. At this time I was in graduate school in Houston, doctoral longings in me, and I wrote Uncle Jeff to offer condolence. His reply is *echt*-cowboy:

Will answer your welcome letter.

Was glad to heare from you again, well it has rained a-plenty here the last week, the grass is good and everything is lovely . . .

Would like for you to visit me, we could talk the things over that we are interested in. What does PhD stand for? to me its post-hole digger, guess that would be about what it would stand for with all the other old Texas cowpokes . . .

I never could understand why a man wanted to spend all his life going to school, ide get to thinking about the Rancho Grandy, and get rambling on my mind, freedom to quote O. M. Roberts:

To what avail the plow or sail or land.

Or life if freedom fail . . .

going to school was always like being in jail to me, life is too short, sweet and uncertain to spend it in jail.

Well, Larry, am still having trouble with my sore eye,

have had it five months now, it looks like pinkeye to me, might have took it from the pink-eyed cow.

Yes it was an awful tragidy to have Mint crushed in the smashup, my car was a total loss too.

Things like that will just hoppen though. It is lonesome dreary out here in the backwoods by myself.

Don't ever join the army, if you do you will have to stay in for four years, that would be a long time to stay in the danged army, this conscription is not according to the constitution of the U.S. its involuntary servitude which is slavery . . .

Well I have just had a couple of Jehovah's witnesses visit me but I soon got them told, I think they are as crazy as a betsie bug and I don't like to be bothered with them, with this sore eye I am in a bad humour most of the time anyway, yours truly

Jeff Dobbs

I doubt that Seneca himself could have balanced the car and the wife that simply, and this about one week after she was gone.

❧

BUT MENTION OF HORSES AND horsemanship brings me back to the McMurtrys, all of whom were devoted to the horse. Indeed, so complete was their devotion that some of them were scarcely competent to move except on horseback. They walk reluctantly and with difficulty, and clearly do not care to be dependent upon their own legs for locomotion. That a person might walk for pleasure is a notion so foreign to them that they can only acquaint it with lunacy or a bad upbringing.

Much as their walking leaves to be desired, it is infinitely to be preferred to their driving. A few of them developed a driver's psychology and a driver's skills, but most of them remained unrepentent horsemen to the end; and an unrepentent horseman at the wheel of a Cadillac is not the sort of person with whom one cares to share a road. That their names are not writ large in the annals of the Highway Patrol is only due to the fact that they lived amid the lightly habited wastes of West Texas and were thus allowed a wider margin of error than most mortals get.

As horsemen their talents varied, but only one or two were without flair. When it came to riding broncs, Jim, the second eldest, was apparently supreme. If he ever saw a horse he was afraid of no one ever knew about it, and in early Archer County his only rival as a bronc-rider was a legendary cowpuncher named Nigger Bones Hook. If the latter's skills were as remarkable as his name he must indeed have been a rider to contend with, but there are those who consider Uncle Jim his equal. Unfortunately, Uncle Jim overmatched himself early in his life and as a consequence was reduced to riding wheelchairs for some forty years. When he was fifteen, William Jefferson let him ride a strong, wild bronc that had been running loose for some years; Uncle Jim stayed on him, but he was not experienced enough to ride him safely and before the ride was over his head was popping uncontrollably. When the horse exhausted himself neither it nor Uncle Jim were able to bring their heads back to a normal position. William Jefferson took both hands and set his son's head straight, but Uncle Jim's neck was broken and he left the field that day with a pinched nerve which would eventually result in a crippling arthritis. Despite the kickback from that one early ride he went on to acquire a large ranch, a wife and family, a couple of banks and a commensurate fortune. The horse that crippled him never raised its head again and died within two days.

When Jim reached the Panhandle in 1900 he was far from done as a rider; indeed, his most celebrated feat was recorded shortly thereafter. He hired on with the ROs, a ranch owned by an extraordinary and very eccentric Englishman named Alfred Rowe, who was later to go down on the *Titanic*. Uncle Jim's wages were fifteen dollars a month. One day Rowe bought seventeen horses from the army, all incorrigibles that had been condemned as too wild to be ridden. Rowe offered Uncle Jim a dollar a head to ride them, and he rode them all that same afternoon, after which, convinced that he had made his fortune, he soon went into business for himself.

Roy McMurtry was apparently the only one of the nine boys to rival Jim's skill with a bucking horse, but few of the others were loath to try their hand (or their seat) with a bronc. It is quite clear that riding was the physical skill most crucially connected with the entrance into manhood. In the spring of 1910 Johnny McMurtry, then still in his teens, borrowed a horse and made his way to the Panhandle, looking for a job as a cowboy. He immediately found one with his brothers Charley and Jim, who were then partners in an operation which at times involved as many as 4,000 cattle. One would have thought that with that many cattle to hassle, a young and extraordinarily willing brother would have been an entirely welcome addition to the staff; but McMurtrys, like most cattlemen, take willingness for granted and judge solely on performance. On almost his first drive Johnny came near to achieving permanent disgrace through a lapse in horsemanship. Some eight hundred nervous yearlings were involved; the older brothers were in the process of calming them after several rather hectic stampedes, one of which had flattened a six wire fence. The cattle were almost quiet when the lapse occurred; the account I quote is from an unpublished memoir left me by Uncle Johnny:

I rode up the bank of Sadler Creek on an old silly horse, he got to pitching and pitched under a cottonwood tree and dragged me off, then into the herd he went and stampeded them again, Jim didn't see it so thought the horse had pitched me off, he caught him and brought him back to me, he was as mad as a gray lobo wolf with hydrophobia, he told me that if I couldn't ride that horse I had better go back to Archer County and catch rabbits for a living, that was about the only horse I had that I could really ride pitching and I was proud of it and was down right insulted for Jim to think I couldn't ride him . . .

The distinction between being drug off and being pitched off might seem obscure to many, but not to a young man whose ego-needs were closely bound up with horsemanship.

✺

AT ANY RATE, ALL THE McMurtrys could ride well enough to get themselves out of Archer County at an early age. Invariably, the direction they rode was northwest, toward the open and still comparatively empty plains of the Panhandle. Specifically they rode to the town of Clarendon, near the Palo Duro canyon, a town which in those days serviced and supplied most of the great Panhandle ranches, among them the JAs and the ROs. For better or worse, Clarendon was their Paris. Charlie arrived in '96, Bob in '99, Jim in 1900, Ed in 1902, Roy in 1920, Lawrence, Grace and May at dates now unremembered, Jo and Jeff in 1916, and Margaret in 1919. Even the old folks went to Clarendon for a time (1919–1925), but doubtless found it impossible to live peacefully with so many of their children about, and soon retreated to the balmier latitudes of Archer County, my father with them.

That that bare and windy little town on the plains should have been so much to my family I find a bit sad, but not inexplicable. Youth is youth and a heyday a heyday, wherever one spends it, and it would appear that at the turn of the century Clarendon was to cowboys what Paris was soon to be for writers. It was the center of the action. If one merely wanted to cowboy, there were the great ranches; and if one was more ambitious the plains was the one place where land in quantity could still be had cheap.

In time the McMurtrys got—and no doubt earned—their share of that land. Most of them started as twenty-dollar-a-month cowboys and quit when they were far enough ahead to buy some land of their own. Seven of the boys and two of the girls lived out their lives within a hundred miles of Clarendon, and in time the nine boys between them owned almost a hundred and fifty thousand acres of Texas land and grazed on it many many thousand head of cattle.

I do not intend here to attempt to describe the McMurtrys one by one. In truth, I didn't know them all that well, not as individuals, and individual character sketches would be neither very interesting nor very authoritative. Most of them were old men when I was very young, and I almost never saw them singly or for any length of time. When I saw them I saw them as a family, grouped with their wives and multitudinous progeny at the family reunions which were held more or less annually from the late forties until the middle sixties. Most of the reunions were held in Clarendon, or, to be more accurate, were held at the Clarendon Country Club, which fact alone is indicative enough of the direction the family had moved.

The Country Club sits some fifteen miles to the northwest of Clarendon, on a ridge not far from the Salt Fork of the Red. Fifteen miles is a short trot in that country and the wives of the local elite would think nothing of driving that far for some minor social function, though as I remember the clubhouse about the only social functions to which it could be adapted were dancing and drinking. Once long ago some cousins and I discovered a couple of rusty slot-machines in a broom closet, indicating that that particular form of gambling had, in those regions at least, passed out of vogue. There was a swimming pool (the one essential of all country clubs), a grove of trees for shade, a windmill for water, and a pond, I suppose, for decor. Of the sights and sounds which one associates with big-city country clubs in Texas—the polished foliage, the liveried staff, the well-parked rows of Mercedes and Lincolns, the tinkle of ice and the ploop of badly hit tennis balls—there was nothing.

Thus, when I saw the McMurtrys, I saw them on the ground that had always held them, the great ring of the plains, with the deep sky and the brown ridges and the restless grass being shaken by the wind as it passed on its long journey from the Rockies south. Teddy Blue mayhap and Old Man Goodnight surely had left their horsetracks on that ridge; there one might have witnessed the coming and going of the god. One by one the old men arrived, in heavy cars with predominantly heavy wives, followed now and then by cautious offspring in Chevrolets. The day was given over to feasting and anecdotage, in almost equal division. The barbecuing was entrusted to a Negro and a County Agent and generally consisted of about a hundred chickens (for the women and youngsters) and a side of beef (for the men, who, being cattlemen, scorned all other meat if beef were available). Vegetables were irrelevant, but there was usually a washpot full of beans, and of course, twenty or thirty cakes brought by the twenty or thirty wives. Later, should the season be opportune, a pickup full of watermelons might arrive, easily sufficient to bloat such children as were not already bloated on soda pop. Gourmandry was encouraged, indeed, almost demanded, and I recall one occasion when the son of someone's hired hand put all the young McMurtrys to shame by consuming twenty-six Dr Peppers in the course of a single day.

In the forenoon the family normally split itself into three groups, the division following the traditional dividing line of Western gatherings: men, women, and children, or each to his own kind. After lunch everyone was too stuffed to move and mingled freely if somewhat heavily. My hundred or so cousins and I found generally that we could do without one another with no ill effects, and in the afternoons I picked my way gingerly among the bulging uncles and aunts, eavesdropping on such conversations as interested me. With most of my uncles I had no rapport at all. To their practiced eye it must have been evident from the first that I was not going to turn out to be a cattleman. For one thing, I wasn't particularly mean, and in the West the mischief quotient is still a popular standard for measuring the appearance of approvable masculine qualitites in a youngster. Any boy worth his salt was expected to be a nuisance, if not to the adults at least to the weaker members of his own age group. I was a weaker member myself; indeed, though I don't remember it, I believe at some early and very primitive reunion I was cast into a hog wallow or pelted with ordure or something; though the atrocity may be apocryphal it would not have been out of keeping with the spirit of such occasions. Mean kids meant strength in time of need, and how could the elders be sure that a bookish and suspiciously observant youngster like myself might not in time disgrace the line? I knew from an early age that I could never meet their standard, and since in those days theirs was the only standard I knew existed I was the more defensive around them. Indeed, scared. One was mild and two were gentle: the rest, with one exception, were neither harder nor softer than saddle leather. The one exception, was, in my estimation, harder than your average saddle. Tolerance was a quality I think no McMurtry ever understood, much less appreciated, and though one or two of them came to understand mercy it was never the family's long suit.

Strength was quite obviously the family's long suit: strength of body, strength of will, and, over it all, strength of character. One of my difficulties with them was that their strength of character was totally and inflexibly committed to a system of values that I found not wholly admirable. The talk beneath the reunion tent was the talk of men whose wills had begun to resent their weakening bodies. They had all, like Hector, been tamers of horses once—adventure and physical hardship had been the very ground of their manhood. The talk was often of the hardships of their youth, hardships that time with its strange craft had turned into golden memories. As I listened and grew older I became, each year, more sharply aware of the irony of the setting: that those men, who in their youth had ridden these same plains and faced their winds and dangers, should in their age buy so puny a symbol as the Clarendon Country Club, the exultantly unbourgeois and undomestic ideal of the Cowboy expiring in the shade of that most bourgeois and most domestic institution. To give them credit, though, I doubt that any of them were happy about it.

Of all the hardship stories I heard, the one which remains most resonant in my mind is the story of the molasses barrel. It was, for all witnesses, a traumatic event. Late one fall, not long after the turn of the century, William Jefferson had gone to the small town of Archer City to purchase the winter's provisions. Archer City was eighteen miles from the ranch, a tedious trip by wagon. He returned late in the afternoon, and among the supplies he brought back was an eighty-pound barrel of good sorghum molasses, in those days the nearest thing to sugar that could be procured. Such sweetening as the family would have for the whole winter was in the barrel, and all gathered around to watch it being unloaded. Two of the boys rolled the barrel to the back of the wagon and two more reached to lift it down, but in the exchange of responsibilities someone failed to secure a hold and the barrel fell to the ground and burst. Eighty pounds of sweetness quivered, spread out, and began to seep unrecoverably into the earth, Grace, the oldest girl, unable to accept the loss, held her breath and made three desperate circles of the house before anyone could recover himself sufficiently to catch her and pound her on the back. Indeed, the story was usually told as a story on Grace, for most of them had suppressed the calamity so effectively that they could not remember how anyone else had responded. They could speak with less emotion of death and dismemberment than of that moment when they stood and watched the winter's sweetness soak into the chicken yard.*

༄

UNCLE JOHNNY, THE SEVENTH BOY, was born in 1891. He was my favorite uncle and in many ways the family's darling, and I should like to write of him in some detail. Of them all, he fought the suburb most successfully, and hewed closest

---

*It now appears that the uncle who first told me this sad story had added a few flowers of his own. What "really happened," it seems, is that the barrel of molasses had a wooden spigot, and was unloaded safely and laid across two support beams so that when the spigot was opened the molasses would drain into the molasses pitcher. Unfortunately, a sow came along one day, walked under the barrel, and rooted the spigot out. The molasses drained from the barrel and ran down a footpath all the way to the lots. The catastrophe was thus discovered and the children lined up beside the path to weep. As with many family stories, I think I prefer the fiction to the truth.

to the nineteenth century ideal of the cowboy. He was the last to be domesticated, if indeed he ever was domesticated, and at one point he almost abandoned the struggle to be a rancher in order to remain a free cowboy. Indeed, according to the memoir he left me, the desire to be a cowboy was his first conscious desire:

> Dad had built two log barns and we boys would climb on top of those barns and watch the herds go by, never since then have I wanted to be anything except a cowboy . . .

By the time he was twelve he could chop cotton well enough to consider himself financially independent, and after only a month or two of labor was able to buy a second-hand saddle. By that time he had completed such textbooks as the little schoolhouse on Idiot Ridge possessed, and he was not again impeded by education until 1909, when Louisa Francis persuaded him to enroll in a business college in McKinney. The school was teeming with chiggers, but Uncle Johnny applied himself grimly and in only four months acquired a diploma stating that he was a Bachelor of Accounts. He was the only McMurtry to achieve such eminence, and was also, ironically, the only McMurty ever to go formally broke.

As soon as his course was finished he had to begin to think about paying for it. He went home, borrowed a horse, and headed for the Panhandle, equipped with his original secondhand saddle and seven dollars in cash. He meant to hire on with the JAs, but stopped by first to visit Charley and Jim at their ranch on the Salt Fork of the Red. They were shrewd men and doubtless knew a good thing when they saw it riding up. They hired him immediately at twenty dollars a month and keep, which meant, apparently, that he was allowed to eat whatever small vermin he could catch.

Not that Uncle Johnny cared: at this time his eagerness for the cowboy life was little short of mystical. He was willing to forgo eating, if necessary, and fortunately had never much liked to sleep either. Fortunately, since to his brothers 3 A.M. was traditionally the end of the night.

He worked for Charley and Jim three years, much of that time in a bachelor camp on the baldies, as the high plains were then called. His possessions consisted of a saddle, shirt, pants, and chaps, two quilts, a six-shooter, and a horse called Sugar-in-the-Gourd. In coolish weather his brothers generously provided him with a tepee, a small stove, and a bucket of sourdough. He spent his wages on cattle—there being nothing else in his vicinity to spend them on—and when his brothers phased him out in 1913 he had paid off the business college and was fifteen hundred dollars to the good.

The yen to work for a really big ranch was still strong in him, so he drifted southwest to the Matadors and hired on with them two days before the wagons pulled out for the spring roundup in 1913. The Matador, like the ROs, was English-owned; they then ran 50,000 head of cattle on slightly over a half-million acres of land. By August Uncle Johnny had helped in the rounding up and shipping of some 19,000 steers, and by early December had assisted in the branding of 11,000 calves.

From the minute he saw the Matador wagons he seemed to realize that he had found his blood's country, and he often said that if he could choose three years to live over they would be the years he had spent with the Matadors. Much of the memoir is devoted to those years, and to the men he worked with: Weary Willie Drace, his wagon-boss, Rang Thornton, Pelada Vivian, and the Pitchfork Kid, names which mean nothing now. In speaking of their departed comrades, men once renowned but soon to be forgotten, old cowboys invariably draw upon the same few images, all of them images taken from their work. Thus, here is Teddy Blue, speaking of the men who had gone with him in the seventies up the long trail to the Yellowstone:

> Only a few of us are left now, and they are scattered from Texas to Canada. The rest have left the wagon and gone ahead across the big divide, looking for a new range. I hope they find good water and plenty of grass. But wherever they are is where I want to go.*

And here, a generation later, is Uncle Johnny, speaking of his buddy the Pitchfork Kid:

> His equal will never be seen on earth again and if he is camping the wagon and catching beeves in the great perhaps and I am fortunate enough to get there I won't be foolish enough to try and run ahead of him and catch the beef, I know it can't be done . . .

By October of 1915 he had increased his savings to $2500 and he decided to take the leap from cowboying to ranching, clearly one of the harder decisions he ever made:

> I left the wagon at the Turtle Hole, I have never before or since hated to do anything as bad as I hated to leave that wagon and to this day when I go down through there I am filled with nostalgia, just looking at the old red hill in Croton, the breaks on the Tongue River and the Roaring Springs, if I had known that leaving was going to be that hard I would have stayed and worn myself out right there . . .

---

* *We Pointed Them North*, p. 230.

Where he went was a ranch in the sandy country south of Muleshoe, near the New Mexico line, and he stayed there the rest of his life. He struggled for more than ten years to keep the first ranch he bought, lost it and went stone broke in 1930, struggled back, and died owning several thousand acres, several hundred cows, and a Cadillac.

❦

I SAW UNCLE JOHNNY'S RANCH for the first time when I was in my early teens and went there for a reunion. Three times in all he managed to capture the reunion for Muleshoe, and for the children of the family those were high occasions, quite different in quality from anything Clarendon offered. To begin with, Uncle Johnny lived far out in the country— and such country. I thought the first time I saw it that only a man who considered himself forsaken of God would live in such country, and nothing I have found out since has caused me to alter that view. The more I saw of it the more I knew that he had been well-punished for casting over the Edenic simplicity of the Matador wagons.

Then too, the house in which he lived, or, at least, in which he might have lived, was a bit out of the ordinary. It was a towering three-story edifice, reminiscent of the house in *Giant*. Every grain of paint had long since been abraded away by the blowing sand. The house had been built by an extremely eccentric New York architect, who must also have considered himself forsaken of God. Indeed, in the long run he probably was, for solitude and his wife's chirpings eventually drove him mad and he came in one morning from chopping wood, called her into the basement, and killed her on the spot with the flat of his axe, or so legend had it. No one had ever bothered to remove the basement carpet, and the spot, or splotch, remained. Nothing could have had a more Dostoevskian impact on such simple Texas kids as we were than that large irregular stain on the basement rug. A good part of every Muleshoe reunion was given over to staring at it, while we mentally or in whispers tried to reconstruct the crime.

When we grew tired of staring at the spot we usually turned our attentions to the player piano. The architect had apparently been as nostalgic for Gotham as Uncle Johnny was for the Matador wagons, since the piano was equipped with duplicate rolls of "The Sidewalks of New York" and a number of other ditties that must have evoked really choking memories amid those wastes. There were also a few spiritual items such as "The Old Rugged Cross," meant, no doubt, for his wife's Bible group. Over the years Uncle Johnny had developed a keen distaste for the piano, or perhaps for the selection of rolls, and he was always dashing in and attempting to lock it, an endeavour in which he was somehow never successful.

He himself appeared not to care for the house, and slept in the little bunk-house. The only sign that he ever inhabited the big house was that the bed in the master bedroom had eleven quilts on it, compensation, no doubt, for having wintered on the baldies with one blanket, one soogan and a wagon sheet. He generally had in his employ a decrepit cook of sorts (male) and one or two desperately inept cowboys, usually Mexican. These slept in the bunkhouse too, or did if they were allowed the leisure to sleep. All the McMurtrys were near-fanatic workers, but Uncle Johnny was by all accounts the most relentless in this regard. His brothers often said, with a certain admiration, that Johnny never had learned how much a horse or a human being could stand. Such humans as worked for him stood as much as he could stand, or else left; and he had to an extraordinary degree that kind of wiry endurance which is fairly common in the cow country. His health broke when he was thirty-three and he was partially crippled the rest of his life, but it hardly seems to have slowed him down. He could not be kept in bed more than five hours a night, and even with one leg virtually useless sometimes branded as many as eight hundred cattle in one day; once, indeed, he vaccinated 730 off the end of a calf-dragger's rope in one afternoon.

In the last ten years of his life he sustained an almost incredible sequence of injuries, one following on another so rapidly that he could scarcely get from one hospital to the next without something nearly fatal happening to him. His arthritis was complicated by the fact that his right leg had been broken numerous times. Horses were always falling with him and on him, or throwing him into trees, or kicking him across corrals. The McMurtrys seemed to consider that these minor injuries were no more than he deserved, for being too tight to buy good horses instead of young half-broken broncs. He appreciated good horses, of course, but when he had something to do would get on any horse that stood to hand. One leg was broken almost a dozen times in such manner and near the end he was so stiff that he had his cowboys wire him on his horses with baling wire, a lunatic thing to do considering the roughness of the country and the temperament of most of the horses he rode.

In the late fifties he got cancer of the throat and had his entire larynx removed. For awhile he spoke with an electric voice-box, a device which rendered his dry, wry wit even dryer and wryer. He soon grew dissatisfied with that, however, and learned to speak with an esophageal voice; it left him clear but barely audible and greatly reduced his effectiveness as a ranconteur. No sooner was he home from the hospital after his throat operation than he got out to shut a gate and let his own pickup run over him, crushing one hip and leg horribly. He managed to dig himself out and crawl back to his ranch, and was immediately flown back to the same hospital.

In time he recovered and went home to Muleshoe and got married, this in his sixty-fifth year. The day after his wedding, so I am told, he and Aunt Ida, his bride, spent some eleven hours horseback, sorting out a herd of cattle he had bought in Lousiana. Two years later, while on their way to Lubbock, a car ran into them on the highway and broke them both up like eggshells. Aunt Ida got a broken back and knee, Uncle Johnny two broken knees and a bad rebreakage of his crippled leg. In time they both recovered but Uncle Johnny was scarcely home before he allowed a whole feed-house full of hundred-pound sacks of cattle feed to fall on top of him, breaking his leg yet again.

In the days of the Muleshoe reunions, most of these disasters were still in the future and he was very much his vigorous self. He owned a Cadillac at this time, but did almost all of his driving in an army surplus jeep of ancient vintage, so ancient, in fact, that it lacked both roof and seats. The small matter of the seat Uncle Johnny took care of by turning a syrup-bucket upside down in the floorboards and balancing a piece of two-by-four across it. This worked well enough for day-to-day driving, but once when he set out to haul a trailerful of pigs to Lubbock the arrangement proved imperfect. The pigs turned over the trailer, the wrench threw Uncle Johnny off the syrup bucket, and jeep, trailer, uncle and swine ended up in a heap in the bar-ditch. He was not much hurt in the accident but was very out of temper before he managed, afoot and with only one usable leg, to get the seven wild pigs rounded up again.

Few of the McMurtrys were devoid of temper and he was not one of those who lacked it, yet I think no child ever sensed his temper. Children found him extraordinarily winning, the perfect uncle and instant confidant. He brought a quality to uncleship that only certain childless men can bring—adult, and yet not domestic. I had always supposed him a truly gentle man and was very shocked, one night, to hear him say that the way to handle Mexicans was to kick loose a few of their ribs every now and then. I had only to reflect on that awhile to realize that I had never known a cowboy who was also a truly gentle man. The cowboy's working life is spent in one sort of violent activity or other; an ability to absorb violence and hardship is part of the proving of any cowboy, and it is only to be expected that the violence will extend itself occasionally from animals to humans, and particularly to those humans that class would have one regard as animals.

One of the more dramatic manifestations of Uncle Johnny's temper occurred just prior to the last of the Muleshoe reunions. For nostalgia's sake he grazed a few animals of even greater vintage than his jeep, among them a large male elk and an aging buffalo bull. The two animals were never on very good terms, and indeed the old buffalo was regarded as a great nuisance by everyone attached to the ranch. A few days before the reunion someone, Uncle Johnny most likely, made the mistake of leaving the elk and the buffalo alone in the same pen for an hour. The two soon joined in battle, and the battle raged freely for quite some time, neither combatant able to gain a clear advantage. When Uncle Johnny happened on the scene, half of his corrals had been flattened and much of the rest knocked hopelessly awry. Enraged, he at once found in favor of the elk and shot the buffalo dead on the spot. An hour later, when he was somewhat cooler, the Scotch took precedence over the Irish in him and he decided that it might be a novelty (as it would certainly be an economy) to barbecue the buffalo and serve him to the clan. He thus set free the fatted calf that had been meant for that fate and had the buffalo towed to the barbecue pit. It was barbecued, I believe, for forty-eight hours and on the day of the reunion its flesh proved precisely consistent with the McMurtry character: neither harder nor softer than saddle leather. How long one should have had to chew it to break down its resistance I did not find out.

There is yet one more story about Uncle Johnny, and it is the story which slides the panel, as Mr. Durrell might put it. We have seen him so far as the dashing young cowboy and the lovable family eccentric, and I should probably have always thought of him in those terms if the last story had not come to me. It came as I left for college and was offered as a safeguard and an admonition.

While still young, Uncle Johnny had the misfortune to catch what in those days was called a social disease. Where he got it one can easily imagine: some grim clapboard house on the plains, with the wind moaning, Model A's parked in the grassless yard, and the girls no prettier than Belle Starr. His condition became quite serious, and had my father not gone with him to a hospital and attended him during a prolonged critical period he might well have died.

Instead, he recovered, and in gratitude gave my father a present. Times were hard and Uncle Johnny poor but the present was a pair of spurs with my father's brand mounted on them in gold—extraordinary spurs for this plain country.

Since then, my father has worn no other spurs, and for a very long time Uncle Johnny took on himself the cloth of penance—the sort of penance appropriate to the faith he held. For all McMurtrys and perhaps all cowboys are essentially pantheists: to them the Almighty is the name of drought, the Good Lord the name of rain and grass. Nature is the only deity they really recognize and nature's order the only order they hold truly sacred.

The most mysterious and most respected part of nature's order was the good woman. Even the most innocent cowboy was scarcely good enough for a good woman, and the cowboy who was manifestly not innocent might never be good enough, however much he might crave one. Instead, he might choose just such a setting as Uncle Johnny chose: a country forsaken of God and women, the rough bunkhouse, the raw horses and the unused mansion, the sandstorms and the blue northers—accoutrements enough for any penance.

At sixty-five he married a woman he had known for a very long time. When he began to court her he discovered, to quote the memoir, that "she was a much better woman than I was entitled to." Even after they married it was some time before he considered himself quite worthy to occupy the same house with her. Perhaps when he did, he let the penance go. Despite the series of injuries, his optimism grew, he bought new land, began to talk of a long-postponed world cruise, and wrote on the last page of his memoir:

I have had my share of fun and am still having it, we have a lot of plans for the future and expect to carry them out . . .

Ruin had not taught him well at all. A short while after the feed fell on him he learned that he had cancer of the colon. From that time on he was in great pain. His will to live never weakened, indeed, seemed to increase, but this time the cancer was inexorable and he died within three years, his world cruise untaken.

❦

IN JULY OF 1965, EIGHT months before he died, Uncle Johnny attended the last reunion. It was held at the Clarendon Country Club, on a fine summer day, and as reunions went, it was a quiet, sparsely attended affair. There was a light turnout of cousins and no more than a dozen or two small children scattered about. The food was catered this time, and just as well, too; the Homeric magnificence of some of the earlier feasts would have been largely wasted on the tired and dyspeptic McMurtrys who managed to drag themselves to the plains that day. Charlie and Jim were dead, several of the others were sick, and most of the survivors had long since ruined their digestions.

The talk was what the talk had always been, only the tones had more audible cracks and the rhythms were shorter. Once I saw Uncle Bob, who was just recovering from a broken hip, trying to talk to Uncle Johnny, who was still recovering from his final broken leg. It was a fine paradigm of the existential condition, for the two brothers were standing on a windy curve of the ridge, moving their mouths quite uselessly. Uncle Johnny had almost no voice and Uncle Bob even less hearing, and indeed, had they been able to communicate they would probably only have got in a fight and injured themselves further, for they were not always in accord and it was rumoured that only a few months earlier they had encountered one another on the streets of Amarillo and almost come to blows.

Uncle Johnny, all day, was in very great pain, and only the talk and the sight of the children seemed to lift him above it. Finally it was three o'clock and the white sun began to dip just slightly in its arch. It was time for he and Aunt Ida to start the two-hundred-mile drive back to Muleshoe. Uncle Johnny reached for his white Stetson and put it on and all of his brothers and sisters rose to help him down the gentle slope to the Cadillac. Most of the women were weeping, and in the confusion of the moment Aunt Ida had forgotten her purse and went back to the tables to get it, while Uncle Johnny, helped by the lame and attended by the halt, worked his way around the open door of the car and stood there a few minutes, kissing his sisters goodbye. Though he was seventy-five and dying there was yet something boyish about him as he stood taking leave of the family. He stood in the frame that had always contained him, the great circular frame of the plains, with the wind blowing the grey hair at his temples and the whole of the Llano Estacado at his back. When he smiled at the children who were near, the pain left his face for a second, and he gave them the look that had always been his greatest appeal—the look of a man who saw life to the last as a youth sees it, and who sees in any youth all that he himself had been.

The family stood awkwardly around the car, looking now at Uncle Johnny, now at the shadow-flecked plains, and they were as close in that moment to a tragic recognition as they would ever be: for to them he had always been the darling, young Adonis, and most of them would never see him alive again. There were no words—they were not a wordy people. Aunt Ida returned with her purse and Uncle Johnny's last young grin blended with his grimace as he began the painful task of fitting himself into the car. In a few minutes the Cadillac had disappeared behind the first brown ridge, and the family was left with its silence and the failing day.

※

THERE, I THINK, THIS BOOK should end: with that place and that group, witnesses both to the coming and going of the god. Though one could make many more observations about the place, about the people, about the myth, I would rather stop there, on the sort of silence where fiction starts. Texas soaks up commentary like the plains soak up a rain, but the images from which fiction draws its vibrancy are often very few and often silent, like those I have touched on in this chapter. The whiskey jug hanging in the barn for nineteen years; the children, rent with disappointment around the puddle of molasses; the whorehouse and the gold-mounted spurs. And Uncle Jeff, alone in the backwoods with his bad eye and his memories of the Rancho Grandy; and Uncle Johnny, riding up the Canadian in 1911 on a horse called Sugar-in-the-Gourd, and, only four years later, riding away bereft from the Roaring Springs, the dream of innocence and fullness never to be redeemed.

Those images, as it happens, all come from Old Texas, but it would not be hard to find in today's experience, or tomorrow's, moments that are just as eloquent, just as suggestive of gallantry or strength or disappointment. Indeed, had I more taste for lawsuits I would list a few for balance. Texas is rich in unredeemed dreams, and now that the dust of its herds is settling the writers will be out on their pencils, looking for them in the suburbs and along the mythical Pecos. And except to paper riders, the Pecos is a lonely and a bitter stream.

I have that from men who rode it and who knew that country round—such as it was, such as it can never be again.

Bibliography

Abbott, E. C. ("Teddy Blue"), and Helena Huntington Smith. *We Pointed Them North*. New York: Farrar and Rinehart, 1939; Norman: University of Oklahoma Press, 1954.

By any standard, a superb memoir; and far and away the best book on the trail-drivers. With Teddy Blue, Haley's biography of Goodnight, Erwin Smith's book of range photographs and a volume of J. R. Williams' cowboy cartoons, one can figure out just about anything one might need to know about the nineteenth century cowboy.

Algren, Nelson. *Somebody in Boots*. New York: Vanguard, 1935. *A Walk on the Wild Side*. New York: Farrar Straus and Cudahy, 1956.

The early sections of both books are set in the lower Rio Grande valley, a region to which Algren still holds the best claim.

Anderson, Edward. *Thieves Like Us*. New York: Stokes, 1937.

The cinema-inspired interest in Clyde Barrow and Bonnie Parker prompts me to include this novel. It suffers from the stylistic flatness which weakens so much Depression fiction, but it is still the most readable treatment the two outlaws have received.

Bedichek, Roy. *Adventures with a Texas Naturalist*. New York: Doubleday, 1947; Austin: University of Texas Press, 1961.

Bainbridge, John. *The SuperAmericans*. New York: Doubleday, 1961.

Berger, Thomas. *Little Big Man*. New York: Dial, 1964.

Brammer, William. *The Gay Place*. Boston: Houghton Mifflin, 1961.

Casey, Bill. *A Shroud for a Journey*. Boston: Houghton Mifflin, 1962.

Dobie, J. Frank. *Tongues of the Monte*. Boston: Little Brown, 1935. *Guide to Life and Literature of the Southwest*. Austin: University of Texas Press, 1943. *Some Part of Myself*. Boston: Little Brown, 1967.

Eastlake, William. *The Bronc People*. New York: Harcourt Brace, 1958. *Portrait of an Artist with 26 Horses*. New York: Simon and Schuster, 1963.

Graves, John. *Goodbye to a River*. New York: Knopf, 1960.

Haley, J. Evetts. *Charles Goodnight: Cowman and Plainsman*. Boston: Houghton Mifflin, 1936; Norman: University of Oklahoma Press, 1949.

Harrison, William. *The Theologian*. New York: Harpers, 1965.

An excellent first novel. Its principal setting is the lower Gulf Coast.

Hickey, Dave. "I'm Bound to Follow the Longhorn Cow." Published in *The Riata*, a student publication of the University of Texas. Austin: 1964.

Hoagland, Edward. "Cowboys" in *The Noble Savage* (1). New York: 1964.

Humphrey, William. *The Ordways*. New York: Knopf, 1965.

Hunter, C. L. (Evangelist). *How God Saved My Buddie in the Eastland County Jail* and *The Tragic Slaying of My First Born*. Ft. Worth: c. 1939.

An essential pamphlet, unfortunately very inaccessible now. The only known copy is in the possession of the poet David Meltzer, of San Francisco.

Leslie, Warren. *Dallas: Public and Private*. New York: Grossman, 1964.

Manfred, Frederick. *Riders of Judgment*. New York: Random House, 1957.

Mann, Dene Hofheinz. *You Be the Judge*. Houston: Premier Printing, 1965.

Valuable, as I said, for page 57.

Malone, William. *The History of Hillbilly Music*. Austin: University of Texas Press, 1968.

I had intended to include an essay on hillbilly music, but the impending publication of Mr. Malone's impressive study made such a chapter unnecessary. If anyone knows more about the subject than he does, God help them.

McCombe, Leonard. *The Cowboy: A Book of Pictures About His Real Life*. New York: Picture Press, 1951. Text by John Bryson.

Olmstead, Frederick Law. *A Journey Through Texas*. New York: Dix Edwards and Co., 1857.

Perhaps the most readable of the nineteenth century travellers.

Smith, Erwin E. and J. Evetts Haley. *Life on the Texas Range*. Austin: University of Texas Press, 1952.

An extraordinarily fine photographic study of cowboy life as it was at the turn of the century.

Stegner, Wallace. "Born Square: The Westerner's Dilemma." *Atlantic*, January 1964; and "Genesis," in *Wolf Willow*, New York: Viking, 1962.

Warshow, Robert. "Movie Chronicle—The Westerner" in *The Immediate Experience*. New York: Doubleday, 1962.

Walker, Stanley. *Home to Texas*. New York: Harpers, 1956.

Webb, Walter Prescott. *The Texas Rangers*. Boston: Houghton Mifflin, 1935; Austin: University of Texas Press, 1965. *The Great Frontier*. Boston: Houghton Mifflin, 1952; Austin: University of Texas Press, 1964.

Williams, J. R. *Why Mothers Get Gray*. New York: Scribners, 1945. *Born Thirty Years Too Soon*. New York: Scribners, 1945. *Kids Out Our Way*. New York: Scribners, 1946. *Cowboys Out Our Way*. New York: Scribners, 1951.